KNITTING NORO

KNITTING NORO

The Magic of Knitting with Hand-Dyed Yarns

JANE ELLISON

POTTER
CRAFT

New York

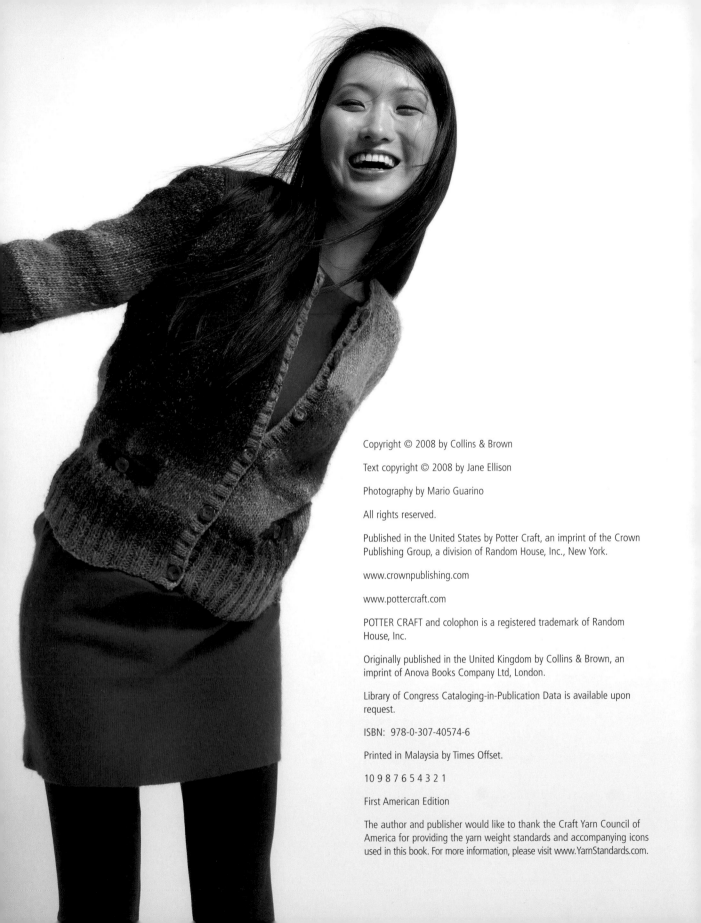

Text copyright © 2008 by Jane Ellison

Photography by Mario Guarino

Published in the United States by Potter Craft, an imprint of the Crown Publishing Group, a division of Random House, Inc., New York.

www.crownpublishing.com

www.pottercraft.com

POTTER CRAFT and colophon is a registered trademark of Random House, Inc.

Originally published in the United Kingdom by Collins & Brown, an imprint of Anova Books Company Ltd, London.

Library of Congress Cataloging-in-Publication Data is available upon request.

ISBN: 978-0-307-40574-6

Printed in Malaysia by Times Offset.

10 9 8 7 6 5 4 3 2 1

First American Edition

The author and publisher would like to thank the Craft Yarn Council of America for providing the yarn weight standards and accompanying icons used in this book. For more information, please visit www.YarnStandards.com.

CONTENTS

introduction

A statement on Noro's website explains their company philosophy: "to produce yarn that is natural and gentle to people and nature. We hope our yarn will provide joy and happiness to people who use it."

This is a great sentence to introduce Noro and my designs, as I also hope that knitting my designs with interesting, enjoyable, and beautiful Noro yarns will bring joy and happiness to those who knit or to those who receive a garment as an everlasting gift of friendship and love.

I love knitting and feel it is something anyone and everyone can do. It isn't difficult or complicated. It is fun and relaxing. Knitting is the ultimate in individual expression.

I have always looked at a knitting pattern as something to change, to adjust to my own personal size or preference. I would see a pattern and change the neckline or the length or on the most basic level, the color. It wasn't until I started working with knitters in a department store that I realized that not all knitters are comfortable altering patterns. I loved helping other knitters choose different colors or advising them on knitting a different length. It was satisfying to see the knitters bring their finished garment in, especially when they were so happy with their work and themselves for creating their own garment.

I like my patterns to be simple and straightforward without confusing techniques, whether you knit them as is or change them to your own personal requirements. This book is the perfect tool to help knitters create their ultimate bespoke garment. Each chapter starts with a basic shape and then, through variations, gently explains how to change sleeve length, necklines, or body length to create a new garment. It also explains how easy it is to substitute yarns within the Noro Yarn Collection, which means the possibilities of garments to knit from this book are endless! The beauty of the simple designs combined with the exciting yarns results in unique additions to any wardrobe, sure to be treasured for years to come.

Jane Ellison

"Enjoy the art at all levels of creation,
the finest fibers from nature at its best,
yarn compositions that read like symphonies,
colors that reflect the life, beauty and mood of our world,
textures as varied as our beloved Earth and its people,
a touch that boasts of luxury, that praises the richness of nature,
and style, fashionable and yet broad in its appeal, style that allows the
knitted fabric to live, to tempt, to excite. Live the Noro experience. Enjoy."

Eisaku Noro

above left: Pure wool is first dyed in an array of vibrant colors.
above center: Colored fibers are manually aligned to make a single yarn.

above right: The beautiful variety of colors and shades is visible in every hank of Noro yarn.

the noro experience

Established by designer Eisaku Noro in the Aichi province of Japan, Noro has for decades been developing yarns made from the finest raw materials imaginable, employing traditional manufacturing processes that mean that Noro yarns have no equal. Now, with the company expanding its distribution into America, Europe, and Southeast Asia, knitters and knitwear designers the world over are discovering the beauty of Noro yarns for themselves. So what exactly is it that makes these particular yarns so special?

First, Noro's technical expertise is unsurpassed. Understanding the physical characteristics of the materials one is working with is essential in any manufacturing process and, in the manufacture of yarns made entirely from natural materials, variations in the source material—the wool—also need to be taken into account. Naturally, different breeds of sheep produce different kinds of wool: a Merino sheep from the southern hemisphere, for example, will create a very different kind of wool than a traditional breed such as a Wensleydale sheep from northern England, where the animal has to withstand cooler climes and harsher weather conditions. That much is obvious—but differences in temperature, humidity, rainfall, grass, the mowing period, and the seasons also have an effect on the wool. As a company, Noro also thoroughly researches the staple length, thickness, weight, expansion, luster, and suppleness of each fiber. Eisaku Noro himself claims to be able to feel those qualities with his eyes shut, by touch alone—an indication of his profound commitment to his subject and his many years' experience as a yarn designer.

Having established all the characteristics of the wool, the second step in creating a yarn is to create a blend that matches the way the yarn will be used. Should it be of a masculine or feminine character? A lightweight fiber that, when knitted up, will drape well or a more robust blend suitable for heavy wear? From the unadulterated luxury of yarns such as Cash Iroha (a blend of silk, lambswool, cashmere, and nylon that drapes exquisitely) to chunky yarns such as Iro (a combination of wool and silk that creates a tweedlike effect when knitted up), Noro's skill in blending fibers is second to none. The effects of these fiber combinations are both visual and tactile: silk, for example, can add depth of color, luster, and smoothness to a yarn, while cashmere and kid mohair contribute soft, fluffy textures. Soft and luxurious to the touch, Noro yarns can transform even the simplest of patterns into something really special.

Next comes the spinning process. Nowadays, almost all spinning is done by machine—but at Noro, machines are used only when the process cannot be done by hand. Eisaku Noro firmly believes that to make something by hand means to make something with love. And, thanks to Noro's spinning method, the company can produce yarn that is 30 to 40 percent lighter than other yarns of the same thickness.

Above all else, however, it is Noro's artistry in blending colors that makes these yarns really stand out. Each ball or hank is individually hand dyed to create a palette that ranges from subtle, gradated shadings to vivid hues of vibrant intensity.

Compare a hank of hand-dyed Noro yarn with a ball of man-made acrylic yarn and the differences between the two are immediately apparent. The acrylic yarn looks flat and dull, a monotone block of unbroken color; the hand-dyed Noro yarn, on the other hand, positively shimmers and sparkles with life. What makes this so appealing is that it replicates, insofar as such a thing is ever possible, the colors of the world around us. Look carefully at any natural object—be it a flower, a leaf, pebbles on a beach, the sea—and you will see that it is not a uniform, solid color. Instead, it is made up of countless tones and shades. Individual cherry blossom petals, for instance, can range from a deep cerise through a delicate blush pink to almost pure white. Pebbles that, at first glance, appear gray may turn out on closer inspection to contain a host of colors from smoky gray to deep charcoal, with inky blues and mossy browns and greens scattered among them for good measure.

This variety is replicated in Noro yarns, with each color blend conjuring up aspects of the natural world from which Eisaku Noro draws his inspiration. (As a yarn designer Eisaku Noro has, for 30 years, been 100 percent committed to the pursuit of colors that depict the vital energy of nature.) A jewel-bright hank of blue-green might evoke images of a tropical reef—but look closer and you will also see soft grays and browns, with moss and lime greens and perhaps even a hint of rust among the azure and aquamarine mixes. Soft blends of green may remind you of a forest in springtime as the trees are just beginning to bud, with undertones of moss and olive green and brown representing the forest floor and splashes of yellow the pale spring sunlight that filters down through the branches. Vibrant reds and oranges, interspersed with splashes of olive green and charcoal, seem to capture the energy and intensity of a flow of molten lava cascading down the sides of a volcano. Offsetting the main colors with tiny accents in this way not only provides visual relief but also prevents the mix from looking flat and monotonous.

Since each yarn is hand dyed, no two hanks are exactly alike, which makes knitting with Noro yarns so exciting. All of these lovely yarns produce fascinating bands of gorgeous colors that change gradually as you knit, making each garment unique.

Creating these wonderful yarns is a repeated process of trial and error. "After hundreds of trials and errors," says Noro, "I might by chance hit on a great result. The materials and time that is spent—sometimes taking up six or seven years to create something really good—is an important part of the process, which I enjoy. I believe that time used in this way will result in something good and beautiful…This is the fundamental of my work…My aim is to make things and at the same time to never forget the origin of the joy of hand-made work."

above left: A web of pure raw wool is produced that is then divided and rolled to produce multi-colored slivers of yarn.

above right: The slivers are then drafted, twisted, and wound onto bobbins ready to be knitted into a truly individual garment.

yarns used in this book

There are two principles that are important to Noro yarns: hand spinning and color.

This hand-spun yarn is made from finely dyed roving. After many years of research, Noro yarns have found the highest quality of dye to produce beautiful and durable colors.

Since most of their yarns are hand spun, the natural luster and texture is preserved. Machinery is used only when necessary at a slow spinning speed by an expert craftsperson. The beauty of the fiber comes from the uneven thickness produced by hand spinning. To appreciate this, Noro asks that you: "please knit gently and discover the joy of knitting with Noro yarns."

As with most yarns, it is important to make sure all your yarn comes from the same dye lot. While two balls from differing lots may look the same, the difference can be very obvious in the knitted fabric. I would recommend buying enough yarn for each project with the same dye lot. However, for the artists out there or those who like to experiment, if you find yourself with extra balls or with odd dye lots, it is easy to mix these within a garment. As the pattern on page 60 shows, you can just knit with a different ball in a stripe.

To the right of each yarn's name you'll see a colored box. These colors indicate which yarns can be easily substituted for one another. As you go through the patterns in this book, use the yarn suggested, or try substituting another yarn of the same type.

SILK GARDEN LITE
シルク ガーデン ライト

Yardage: 137 yds (125m)
Fiber Content: 45% Silk/45% Mohair/ 10% Lambswool
Stitches: 5.5
Needle Size: 6
Weight: 1¾ oz (50g)
(3) light

A "little sister" to Silk Garden, this has the same blend but is a light worsted weight, which makes it perfect for scarves and shawls. The mix of silk, mohair, and lambswool combines lightness with strength and intense color with natural colors. The result is many variegated shades in true Noro style.

CASHMERE ISLAND □
カシュミア アイランド

SILK GARDEN □
シルク ガーデン

KUREYON □
クレヨン

Yardage: 110 yds (100m)
Fiber Content: 60% Wool/
30% Cashmere/10% Nylon
Stitches: 5.5
Needle Size: 6
Weight: 1½ oz (40g)
(3) light

This beautiful Noro yarn feels like pure cashmere. The light worsted weight means it is great for substituting in patterns that call for Silk Garden Lite to give a more luxurious feel to scarves and shawls. Noro's philosophy of beautiful colors that have a strong luster and richness of quality is definitely apparent in Cashmere Island.

Yardage: 122 yds (111.5m)
Fiber Content: 45% Silk/45% Mohair/
10% Lambswool
Stitches: 4.5
Needle Size: 7-8
Weight: 1¾ oz (50g)
(4) medium

The Silk Garden yarn is an excellent partner to Kureyon as it is also a worsted weight. The silk in this yarn absorbs colors creating bright vivid shades, while the mix of mohair and lambswool soften the intensity to create a lovely natural feel. This is a variegated yarn that has many popular colors including some classic bestsellers.

Yardage: 110 yds (100m)
Fiber Content: 100% wool
Stitches: 4.5
Needle Size: 7-8
Weight: 1¾ oz (50g)
(4) medium

This is one of the most popular Noro yarns. It is 100% wool in a worsted aran weight. The Kureyon softens on its first wash and feels lovely and warm next to the skin. It is the perfect yarn for felting to create an extra dense fiber that wears well.

Kureyon is produced in a wide variety of beautiful colors, which means that there is more than one favorite shade for everyone.

CASH IROHA
キャッシュ イロハ

KOCHORAN
コチョーラン

IRO
イロ

Yardage: 100 yds (91.5m)
Fiber Content: 40% Silk/30%
Lambswool/20% Cashmere/10% Nylon
Stitches: 4.5
Needle Size: 7-8
Weight: 1½ oz (40g)

 medium

Cash Iroha adds a touch of luxury to the solid shades in the worsted weight. The little bit of nylon gives the yarn strength so it is easy to knit with. The blend of cashmere and silk means it has an amazing sheen and beautiful, soft feel. It is perfect to create solid color garments or to mix with Silk Garden and Kureyon in stripes.

Yardage: 176 yds (160m)
Fiber Content: 50% Wool/30%
Angora/20% Silk
Stitches: 4
Needle Size: 10
Weight: 3½ oz (100g)

4 medium

In Kochoran, Noro once again creates a perfect blend. The angora gives the most luxurious, fluffy, soft feel to this thick worsted yarn and makes it perfect for snuggling up with on winter evenings, while the silk gives the most intense colors. The wool adds balance and strength.

Yardage: 131 yds (120m)
Fiber Content: 75% Wool/25% Silk
Stitches: 3
Needle Size: 10-11
Weight: 3½ oz (100g)

5 chunky

The perfect blend of silk and wool makes this chunky yarn a great favorite. Noro yarn is made by carefully selecting materials and removing all the impurities in the raw wool by hand and without the use of chemicals or machines. Iro certainly shows this with the beautiful smoothness and feel of the yarn. The silk gives the yarn a wonderful intensity of color.

additional yarns that can be substituted

SILVER THAW
シルバー　サウ

NIJI
ニジ

SILK GARDEN CHUNKY
シルク ガーデン チャンキー

Yardage: 232 yds (212m)
Fiber Content: 50% Wool/25% Angora/25% Semi-Cashmere Nylon
Stitches: 4.5
Needle Size: 7-8
Weight: 3½ oz (100g)
4 medium

Silver Thaw is a worsted weight yarn with a blend of angora that gives it a soft, fluffy look. The feel is gentle and soft. Due to the hand spun nature of Noro yarns, in some places the yarn has an uneven thickness. This is especially true with Silver Thaw.

Yardage: 96 yds (88m)
Fiber Content: 45% Wool/25% Silk/25% Kid Mohair/5% Nylon
Stitches: 4
Needle Size: 8
Weight: 1½ oz (40g)
4 medium

This blend from Noro has a totally uniqe look. This is a fancy worsted yarn that uses luxurious fibers to create a fuzzy texture. This yarn can be substituted for Kochoran but the knitter should be aware that the feel, texture, and look will be quite different.

Yardage: 132 yds (120m)
Fiber Content: 45% Silk/45% Mohair/10% Lambswool
Stitches: 3
Needle Size: 10-11
Weight: 1¾ oz (50g)
5 chunky

Another addition to the Silk Garden family, this time in a chunky weight. This is a perfect substitute for Iro, with a softer feel and a more delicate drape.

reading the patterns

SKILL LEVEL
Most knitting books include an indicator of skill level to let the knitter know whether the garment is for the beginner or the more advanced. I have mentioned this information first because there is only one skill level in my book: beginner!

I love knitting just as much as I love the satisfaction of creating my own bespoke garments. You do not have to be an advanced knitter to create a one-of-a-kind piece. With this in mind I want other people to share my joy of knitting. My patterns are simple, straightforward, and easy to follow, which results in a beautiful classic garment. They work perfectly with the Noro yarns.

Each design begins with a basic silhouette, followed by five variations. If you like a certain silhouette—a cardigan, for example—you can knit this with a v-neck or crew neck, with short sleeves or long sleeves, and you don't have to write out the pattern or work out the math. Just follow my pattern.

MEASUREMENTS AND SIZING INFORMATION
Everyone is unique and no two people have the same body size. Before starting your garment, please check the "Actual Measurement" to make sure you are making the perfect size.

Each pattern includes a measurement "To Fit Chest" and an "Actual Measurement." The "Actual Measurement" shows the finished garment's length and width. Once you have chosen the garment you wish to knit, find a similar garment in your wardrobe that fits you well. Lay your existing garment out flat and measure across the chest (about 1" (2cm) under the armholes). Once you have this figure, compare it to the width measurements in the pattern and choose the knitted garment size that is nearest to this figure.

MAKING YOUR BESPOKE GARMENT
The patterns in the book lead you through making your own bespoke garment, so one pattern can be knitted with a v-neck or a round neck, with short sleeves or with long sleeves. With my patterns and the beautiful Noro yarn there are endless possibilities and the satisfying knowledge that there will never be another garment like yours in the world, even if another knitter (or yourself) used exactly the same yarn and pattern.

However, if you wanted to lengthen or shorten the garment to another measurement, the best place to do this is in the instructions before you start to shape the armholes. Ask a friend to measure your back from the top of your shoulder to your desired length. Compare this length with the one in the pattern. If you want your garment to be 4" (10cm) longer, knit an additional 4" (10cm) before you shape the armholes. For example, if the pattern says, "Starting with a knit row, continue in stockinette stitch until back measures 12" (30cm) from cast on edge" then change this measurement to 16" (40cm). Don't forget to do this on the front too!

The same principle applies to the sleeves. Once you have knitted the back and front, pin or sew the shoulders together. Pin the side seams and put the garment shell on. Ask a friend to measure from the seam under the arm to your desired length. To lengthen or shorten the sleeve, find the instruction in the pattern that states to "Continue in pattern without shaping until sleeve measures your desired sleeve length from cast on edge," and use your preferred measurement. Remember when making your bespoke garment that you may need more or less yarn than stated.

GAUGE
This is the most important step in making a garment but is also a simple and easy step. Knit a gauge swatch before commencing every pattern.

Every pattern has its own unique gauge which should be measured over a 4" (10cm) square. For an accurate measurement, it's best to make a slightly bigger swatch so you can avoid measuring over any wobbly edges.

To make a gauge swatch, first cast on the amount of stitches stated in the gauge part of the pattern, then cast on an extra 4 stitches. Work in the pattern specified until the square measures 4¾" (12cm). Don't cast off but instead break off the yarn and thread through the stitches, taking them off the needle.

To count your gauge swatch, lay it down flat, perhaps pinned in place. In stockinette stitch, each stitch makes a "V" shape. Place a pin by the side of one stitch and measure 4" (10cm) horizontally with a tape measure, marking this spot with another pin. Count the stitches between the pins. Laying a straight edge along the row will make them easier to count. To count the rows, place your tape measure and pins vertically and do the same.

If you have the stated amount of stitches and rows between the pins you have the correct gauge and can begin your chosen pattern.

If you have too many stitches, your gauge is tight and your garment will be smaller than stated. Change to a larger needle. If there are too few stitches, your gauge is loose and your garment will be bigger than stated. Change to a smaller needle. Always repeat the process until you achieve the correct gauge.

finishing techniques

Many knitters see the finishing or sewing together of the knitted garment as the tedious part of producing your very own garment. However, finishing your garment can be very exciting! There is a simple technique to use that can make sewing up fun. This is called mattress stitch and is explained below. But before sewing it up, you should press and block your work. This is important to do to obtain the correct size.

BLOCKING AND PRESSING
With the right side of the garment face-down on the ironing board, and the wrong side facing up, pin out the garment, making sure the measurements are correct to the pattern. Depending on your iron, gently steam the garment or use the wool setting over a damp cloth, taking extra care not to flatten the texture too much.

Leave the garment to rest for a short while.

MATTRESS STITCH
To sew the garment's sides together you can use back stitch. However, I find mattress stitch more enjoyable and effective.

Lay the pieces right side up next to each other. Work up the column between the edge stitch and the next stitch on each edge—you will lose the edge stitch from each side to make the seam. Put your needle in between the edge and next stitch on one side and pick up two bars. This is your first sewn stitch. Move over to the other piece and do the same. Go back to the point where your needle exited on the first piece and put the

needle back in, finding the next two bars. Continue going back and forth and pulling the thread tight each time. You will see that the two edges are pulled together. Done well, you will hardly notice the join!

SEWING IN ENDS
Once your garment has been sewn together the yarn ends need to be sewn into the seams. Thread the yarn ends through a darning needle and then weave into the seam. Cut the end of the yarn.

WASHING INSTRUCTIONS
On the first wash your Noro garment will soften and if washed carefully your Noro garment will last for years to come. For optimum results turn the garment inside out and gently hand wash in lukewarm water, preferably using a wool detergent. Rinse thoroughly. To remove excess water after washing, roll the garment inside a large towel and very gently squeeze out the excess water.

Dry your garment flat, out of direct sunlight and away from a heat source like a radiator. Gently pull back into shape while damp.

Pressing should be done gently with a steam iron (or on the wool setting over a damp cloth).

TANK TOPS

basic tank

Working with Noro's variegated yarns is always full of surprises—you never quite know what to expect with the striping due to the nature of the yarn. This bold scoopneck tank features modest detailing such as a rolled neckline and hem.

YARN TYPES

YARN
5 (6, 6, 7, 7) balls of Noro Silk Garden, 45% silk/45% mohair/10% lambswool, 1¾ oz (50g), each approximately 110 yds (100m), shade 84 (4️) medium

NEEDLES
One pair size 8 (5mm) knitting needles or size needed to obtain gauge
One pair size 7 (4.5mm) knitting needles

GAUGE
18 stitches and 24 rows to 4" (10cm) square over stockinette stitch using size 8 (5mm) needles.

MEASUREMENTS
to fit chest

30–32	32–34	34–36	36–38	40–42 inches
76–81	81–86	86–91.5	91.5–96.5	101.5–106.5cm

actual measurement

34	35¾	37½	41	43 inches
86.5	91	95.5	104.5	109cm

length

21½	21½	22	22	22½ inches
55	55	56	56	57cm

1

BACK

With size 8 (5mm) needles, cast on 78 (82, 86, 94, 98) stitches. Starting with a knit row, continue in stockinette stitch until the back measures 13¼" (34cm) from the cast-on edge, ending with a wrong-side row.

SHAPE ARMHOLES

Bind off 4 stitches at the beginning of the next 2 rows—70 (74, 78, 86, 90) stitches.

Decrease 1 stitch at each end of the next row. Then decrease 1 stitch at each end of every 4th row twice—64 (68, 72, 80, 84) stitches.

Decrease 1 stitch at each end of the next row. Then decrease 1 stitch at each end of every other row twice—58 (62, 66, 74, 78) stitches.

Continue without shaping in stockinette stitch until the armhole measures 8¼ (8¼, 8½, 8½, 9)" (21 [21, 22, 22, 23]cm) from the start of the armhole shaping, ending with a wrong-side row.

SHAPE SHOULDERS

Bind off 10 (12, 13, 17, 18) stitches at the beginning of the next 2 rows.

Leave the center 38 (38, 40, 40, 42) stitches on a holder.

FRONT

Work as for the Back until the start of the armhole shaping, ending with a wrong-side row.

SHAPE ARMHOLE AND LEFT NECK

Next row Bind off 4 stitches, knit until there are 22 (24, 25, 29, 30) stitches on your needle, slip the remaining 52 (54, 57, 61, 64) stitches onto a holder, turn.

Decrease 1 stitch at each end of the next row. Then decrease 1 stitch at each end of every 4th row twice, then every other row three times—10 (12, 13, 17, 18) stitches.

Continue without shaping in stockinette stitch until the armhole measures 8¼ (8¼, 8½, 8½, 9)" (21 [21, 22, 22, 23]cm) from the start of the armhole shaping, ending with a wrong-side row. Bind off.

SHAPE RIGHT NECK

With right side facing, leaving the center 26 (26, 28, 28, 30) stitches on a holder, rejoin the yarn to the remaining stitches and knit to end.

Purl one row.

Decrease 1 stitch at each end of the next row. Then decrease 1 stitch at each end of every 4th row twice, then every other row 3 times—10 (12, 13, 17, 18) stitches.

Continue without shaping in stockinette stitch until the armhole measures 8¼ (8¼, 8½, 8½, 9)" (21 [21, 22, 22, 23]cm) from the start of the armhole shaping, ending with a wrong-side row. Bind off.

NECK

Join the right shoulder seam. With right side facing and size 7 (4.5mm) needles, pick up and k35 (37, 38, 39, 41) stitches down the left neck, k26 (26, 28, 28, 30) stitches from the holder at the center front, pick up and k35 (37, 38, 39, 41) stitches up the right front neck and knit across 38 (38, 40, 40, 42) stitches from the holder at the center back—134 (138, 144, 146, 154) stitches.

Knit two rows.

Bind off.

ARMHOLE EDGING

Join the left shoulder seam and neck edging. With right side facing and size 7 (4.5mm) needles, pick up and k40 (40, 42, 42, 45) stitches up one armhole edge, pick up and k40 (40, 42, 42, 45) stitches along the other side—80 (80, 84, 84, 90) stitches.

Knit two rows.

Bind off.

FINISHING

Join the side seams.

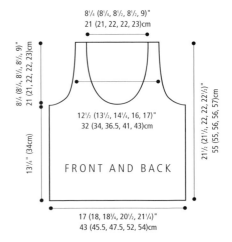

8¼ (8¼, 8½, 8½, 9)"
21 (21, 22, 22, 23)cm

8¼ (8¼, 8½, 8½, 9)"
21 (21, 22, 22, 23)cm

12½ (13½, 14¼, 16, 17)"
32 (34, 36.5, 41, 43)cm

21½ (21½, 22, 22, 22½)"
55 (55, 56, 56, 57)cm

13¼ (34cm)

FRONT AND BACK

17 (18, 18¾, 20½, 21¼)"
43 (45.5, 47.5, 52, 54)cm

v-neck tank

A classic tank is an essential for any contemporary wardrobe and this version is no exception. The variegated yarn transforms a basic style into a fresh and colorful design, while easy stockinette stitch makes for fuss-free knitting. With a relaxed fit, this style works equally well as a layering piece or on its own.

YARN TYPES

YARN
5 (6, 6, 7, 7) balls of Noro Silk Garden, 45% silk/45% mohair/10% lambswool, 1¾ oz (50g), each approximately 110 yds (100m), shade 84 **(4)** medium

NEEDLES
One pair size 8 (5mm) knitting needles or size needed to obtain gauge
One pair size 7 (4.5mm) knitting needles

GAUGE
18 stitches and 24 rows to 4" (10cm) square over stockinette stitch using size 8 (5mm) needles.

MEASUREMENTS
to fit chest

30–32	32–34	34–36	36–38	40–42 inches
76–81	81–86	86–91.5	91.5–96.5	101.5–106.5cm

actual measurement

34	35¾	37½	41	43 inches
86.5	91	95.5	104.5	109cm

length

21½	21½	22	22	22½ inches
55	55	56	56	57cm

BACK
Work as for Basic Tank Back (page 23).

FRONT
Work as for Basic Tank Back (page 23) until the start of the armhole shaping, ending with a wrong-side row.

SHAPE ARMHOLE AND LEFT NECK
Next row Bind off 4 stitches, work until there are 35 (37, 39, 43, 45) stitches on your needle, slip the remaining 39 (41, 43, 47, 49) stitches onto a holder, turn.
Purl 1 row.
Decrease 1 stitch at armhole edge. Then decrease 1 stitch at armhole edge every 4th row twice, then every other row 3 times; **at the same time** decrease 1 stitch at the neck edge of the next and every other row until 10 (12, 13, 17, 18) stitches remain.
Continue without shaping in stockinette stitch until the armhole measures 8¼ (8¼, 8½, 8½, 9)" (21 [21, 22, 22, 23]cm) from the start of the armhole shaping, ending with a wrong-side row.
Bind off.

SHAPE RIGHT NECK
With right side facing, rejoin the yarn to the remaining stitches and knit to end.
Purl 1 row.
Decrease 1 stitch at armhole edge. Then decrease 1 stitch at armhole edge every 4th row twice, then every other row 3 times; **at the same time** decrease 1 stitch at the neck edge of the next and every other row until 10 (12, 13, 17, 18) stitches remain.
Continue without shaping in stockinette stitch until the armhole measures 8¼ (8¼, 8½, 8½, 9)" (21 [21, 22, 22, 23]cm) from the start of the armhole shaping, ending with a wrong-side row.
Bind off.

ARMHOLE EDGING
Join both shoulder seams. Work as for Basic Tank Armhole Edging (page 23).

FINISHING
Join the side seams.

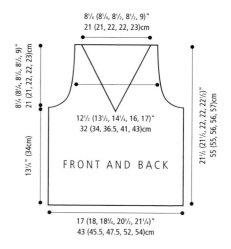

8¼ (8¼, 8½, 8½, 9)"
21 (21, 22, 22, 23)cm

8¼ (8¼, 8½, 8½, 9)"
21 (21, 22, 22, 23)cm

13¾" (34cm)

12½ (13½, 14¼, 16, 17)"
32 (34, 36.5, 41, 43)cm

21½ (21½, 22, 22, 22½)"
55 (55, 56, 56, 57)cm

FRONT AND BACK

17 (18, 18¾, 20½, 21¼)"
43 (45.5, 47.5, 52, 54)cm

3

striped tunic

A striped, chevron pattern throughout the bodice offers a new lease on life to this classic design. Deceptively easy to knit in gorgeous Kureyon, the chevron pattern can be extended and *voilà*—a top that works day to night with ease and grace.

YARN TYPES

YARN

3 (4, 4, 4, 5) balls of Noro Kureyon, 100% wool, 1¾ oz (50g), each approximately 110 yds (100m), shade 154 (A) **(4)** medium

3 (4, 4, 4, 5) balls of Noro Kureyon, 100% wool, 1¾ oz (50g), each approximately 110 yds (100m), shade 182 (B) **(4)** medium

NEEDLES

One pair size 8 (5mm) knitting needles or size needed to obtain gauge
One pair size 7 (4.5mm) knitting needles

GAUGE

18 stitches and 24 rows to 4" (10cm) square over stockinette stitch using size 8 (5mm) needles.

MEASUREMENTS

to fit chest

30–32	32–34	34–36	36–38	40–42 inches
76–81	81–86	86–91.5	91.5–96.5	101.5–106.5cm

actual measurement

34	35¾	37½	41	43 inches
86.5	91	95.5	104.5	109cm

length

28	28	28½	28½	28¾ inches
71	71	72	72	73cm

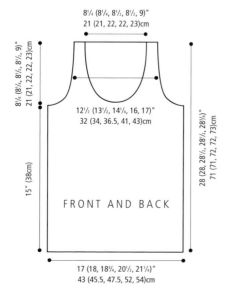

8¼ (8¼, 8½, 8½, 9)"
21 (21, 22, 22, 23)cm

8¼ (8¼, 8½, 8½, 9)"
21 (21, 22, 22, 23)cm

12½ (13½, 14¼, 16, 17)"
32 (34, 36.5, 41, 43)cm

28 (28, 28½, 28½, 28¾)"
71 (71, 72, 72, 73)cm

15" (38cm)

FRONT AND BACK

17 (18, 18¾, 20½, 21¼)"
43 (45.5, 47.5, 52, 54)cm

4-ROW STRIPED PATTERN

Work 2 rows with B.
Work 2 rows with A.
These 4 rows form the striped pattern; repeat throughout.

BACK

With size 8 (5mm) needles and A, cast on 84 (91, 93, 104, 106) stitches.

1st pattern row (right side) K3 (0, 1, 0, 1), [m1 by knitting into the front and back of next stitch, k4, sl, k2tog, psso, k4, m1] to last 3 (0, 1, 0, 1) stitch(es), knit to end.
2nd pattern row Purl.
These 2 rows form the chevron pattern.
Repeat the last 2 rows and the striped pattern until the back measures 14¾" (38cm) from the cast on edge, ending with a right-side row.
Decrease row P2tog 0 (1, 0, 1, 0) times, p9 (3, 7, 3, 7), p2tog, [p11, p2tog] to last 8 (6, 6, 6, 6) stitches, p8 (4, 6, 4, 6), [p2tog] 0 (1, 0, 1, 0) times—78 (82, 86, 94, 98) stitches.
Starting with a knit row, continue in stockinette stitch and striped pattern until the back measures 19¾" (50cm) from the cast-on edge, ending with a wrong-side row.

SHAPE ARMHOLES

Complete as for Basic Tank Back from Shape Armholes (page 23), working in stockinette stitch and striped pattern throughout.

FRONT

Work as for the Back until the start of the armhole shaping, ending with a wrong-side row.

SHAPE ARMHOLES

Complete as for Basic Tank Front from Shape Armhole and Left Neck section (page 23), working in stockinette stitch and striped pattern throughout.

NECK

Work as for Basic Tank Neck (page 23) with A.

ARMHOLE EDGING

Work as for Basic Tank Armhole Edging (page 23) with A.

FINISHING

Join the side seams.

ribbed vest

Layered over a turtleneck and paired with jeans, this carefree design is chic and understated. The vest knits quick and easy with an allover 2x2 rib pattern. The result? A smart figure-flattering design that fits a wide range of body types.

YARN TYPES

YARN
5 (6, 6, 7, 7) balls of Noro Silk Garden, 45% silk/45% mohair/10% lambswool, 1¾ oz (50g), each approximately 110 yds (100m), shade 264 (4) medium

NEEDLES
One pair size 8 (5mm) knitting needles or size needed to obtain gauge

GAUGE
18 stitches and 24 rows to 4" (10cm) square over rib when slightly stretched using size 8 (5mm) needles.

MEASUREMENTS

to fit chest

30–32	32–34	34–36	36–38	40–42 inches
76–81	81–86	86–91.5	91.5–96.5	101.5–106.5cm

actual measurement

34	35¾	37½	41	43 inches
86.5	91	95.5	104.5	109cm

length

21½	21½	22	22	22½ inches
55	55	56	56	57cm

BACK
With size 8 (5mm) needles, cast on 78 (82, 86, 94, 98) stitches.
1st rib row K2, [p2, k2] to end.
2nd rib row P2, [k2, p2] to end.
These 2 rows form the rib pattern.
Repeat the last 2 rows until the Back measures 13¼" (34cm) from the cast-on edge, ending with a wrong-side row.

SHAPE ARMHOLES
Complete as for Basic Tank Back from Shape Armholes (page 23), working in rib pattern throughout and decreasing 1 stitch at the armhole edge, but 4 stitches in from the armhole edge.

FRONT
Work as for the Back until the start of the armhole shaping, ending with a wrong-side row.

SHAPE ARMHOLES
Complete as for Basic Tank from Shape Armhole and Left Neck (page 23), working in rib pattern throughout. Decrease at the neck edge but 7 stitches in from the edge, and at the armhole edge 4 stitches in from the armhole edge.

FINISHING
Join the shoulder seams. Join the side seams.

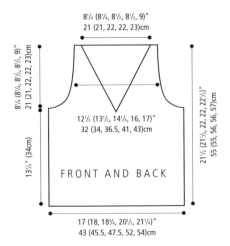

8¼ (8¼, 8½, 8½, 9)"
21 (21, 22, 22, 23)cm

8¼ (8¼, 8½, 8½, 9)"
21 (21, 22, 22, 23)cm

12½ (13½, 14¼, 16, 17)"
32 (34, 36.5, 41, 43)cm

13¼" (34cm)

21½ (21½, 22, 22, 22½)"
55 (55, 56, 56, 57)cm

FRONT AND BACK

17 (18, 18¾, 20½, 21¼)"
43 (45.5, 47.5, 52, 54)cm

YARN

4 (5, 5, 5, 6) balls of Noro Kureyon, 100% wool, 1¾ oz (50g), each approximately 110 yds (100m), shade 40 (A) **④** medium

4 (5, 5, 5, 6) balls of Noro Kureyon, 100% wool, 1¾ oz (50g), each approximately 110 yds (100m), shade 182 (B) **④** medium

NEEDLES

One pair size 8 (5mm) knitting needles or size needed to obtain gauge
One pair size 7 (4.5mm) knitting needles

GAUGE

18 stitches and 24 rows to 4" (10cm) square over stockinette stitch using size 8 (5mm) needles

MEASUREMENTS

to fit chest

30–32	32–34	34–36	36–38	40–42 inches
76-81	81–86	86–91.5	91.5–96.5	101.5–106.5cm

actual measurement

34	35¾	37½	41	43 inches
86.5	91	95.5	104.5	109cm

length

24	24	24½	24½	24¾ inches
61	61	62	62	63cm

turtleneck tank

5

A simple silhouette with no shaping and a garter-stitched turtleneck—this style has the elements of a fashion classic. However, cheerful stripes in saturated hues make it fresh and exciting and elevates the design to a new level, making it one of my personal favorites.

12-ROW STRIPED PATTERN

Work 6 rows in A.

Work 6 rows in B.

These 12 rows form the striped pattern; repeat throughout.

BACK

With size 8 (5mm) needles and A, cast on 78 (82, 86, 94, 98) stitches.

Starting with a knit row, continue in striped pattern and stockinette stitch until the Back measures 15¾" (40cm) from the cast-on edge, ending with a wrong-side row.

SHAPE ARMHOLES

Complete as for Basic Tank Back from Shape Armholes (page 23), working in stockinette stitch and striped pattern throughout.

FRONT

Work as for the Back until armhole measures 5 (5, 5½, 5½, 6)" (13 [13, 14, 14, 15]cm), ending with a wrong-side row.

SHAPE ARMHOLES

Complete as for Basic Tank Back from Shape Armholes (page 23).

SHAPE LEFT NECK

Next row K16 (18, 19, 23, 24) stitches, turn and slip the remaining stitches onto a holder.

Decrease one stitch at the neck edge of the next and every following row until 10 (12, 13, 17, 18) stitches remain.

Continue without shaping in stockinette stitch until the armhole measures 8¼ (8¼, 8½, 8½, 9)" (21 [21, 22, 22, 23]cm) from the start of the armhole shaping, ending with a wrong-side row. Bind off.

SHAPE RIGHT NECK

With right side facing, leave the center 26 (26, 28, 28, 30) stitches on a holder, rejoin the yarn to the remaining stitches, knit to end.

Decrease 1 stitch at the neck edge of the next and every following row until 10 (12, 13, 17, 18) stitches remain. Continue without shaping in stockinette stitch until the armhole measures 8¼ (8¼, 8½, 8½, 9)" (21 [21, 22, 22, 23]cm) from the start of the armhole shaping, ending with a wrong-side row. Bind off.

TURTLENECK

Join the right shoulder seam. With right side facing, using size 7 (4.5mm) needles and A, pick up and k16 (16, 18, 18, 20) stitches down the left neck, k26 (26, 28, 28, 30) stitches from the holder at the center front, pick up and k16 (16, 18, 18, 20) stitches up the right front neck and knit across 38 (38, 40, 40, 42) stitches from the holder at the center back—96 (96, 104, 104, 112) stitches

Starting with a knit row, continue in garter stitch until the turtleneck measures 7" (18cm), ending with a wrong-side row. Bind off loosely.

ARMHOLE EDGING

Join the left shoulder seam and neck edging. Work as for Basic Tank Armhole Edging (page 23) with A.

FINISHING

Join the side seams.

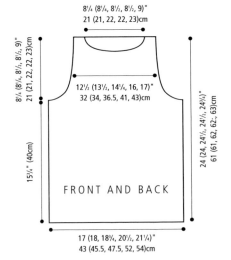

8¼ (8¼, 8½, 8½, 9)"
21 (21, 22, 22, 23)cm

8¼ (8¼, 8½, 8½, 9)"
21 (21, 22, 22, 23)cm

12½ (13½, 14¼, 16, 17)"
32 (34, 36.5, 41, 43)cm

24 (24, 24½, 24½, 24¾)"
61 (61, 62, 62, 63)cm

15¼" (40cm)

FRONT AND BACK

17 (18, 18¼, 20½, 21¼)"
43 (45.5, 47.5, 52, 54)cm

basic chunky cardigan

1

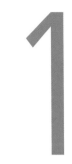

Boy meets girl—designing a chunky cardigan that's bulky and warm yet feminine can be a challenge. This basic stockinette-stitched design has drop shoulders and rolled hems, and wooden buttons add an earthy comfort. In chunky Iro, it knits up faster than you can imagine!

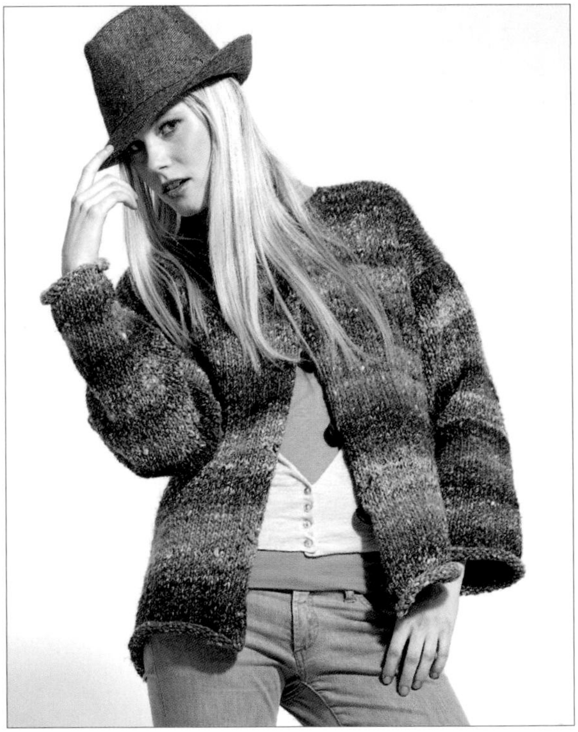

YARN TYPES

YARN

7 (8, 8, 9, 9) balls of Noro Iro, 75% wool/25% silk, 3½ oz (100g), each approximately 131 yds (123m), shade 8 5 chunky

6 buttons size 1¼" (3cm)

NEEDLES

One pair size 10.5 (7mm) knitting needles or size needed to obtain gauge

One pair size 10 (6mm) knitting needles

GAUGE

12 stitches and 18 rows to 4" (10cm) square over stockinette stitch using size 10.5 (7mm) needles.

MEASUREMENTS

to fit chest

32–34	36–38	40–42	44–46	48–50 inches
81–86	91.5–96.5	101.5–106.5	111.5–117	122–127cm

actual measurement

45¾	48½	51	53¾	56½ inches
116.5	123.5	130	136.5	143.5cm

length

24½	24½	24½	25¼	25¼ inches
62	62	62	64	64cm

sleeve length

17¾	17¾	17¾	17¾	17¾ inches
45	45	45	45	45cm

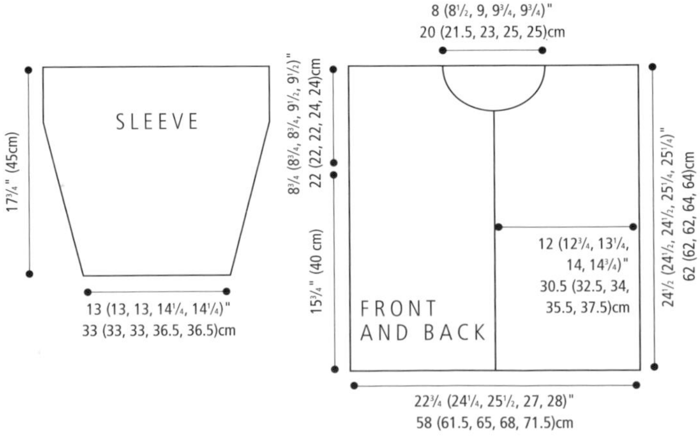

SLEEVE
17¾" (45cm)
13 (13, 13, 14¼, 14¼)"
33 (33, 33, 36.5, 36.5)cm
8 (8½, 9, 9¾, 9¾)"
20 (21.5, 23, 25, 25)cm
8¾ (8¾, 8¾, 9½, 9½)"
22 (22, 22, 24, 24)cm
15¾" (40 cm)
12 (12¾, 13¼, 14, 14¾)"
30.5 (32.5, 34, 35.5, 37.5)cm
FRONT AND BACK
24½ (24½, 24½, 25¼, 25¼)"
62 (62, 62, 64, 64)cm
22¾ (24¼, 25½, 27, 28)"
58 (61.5, 65, 68, 71.5)cm

BACK

With size 10.5 (7mm) needles, cast on 70 (74, 78, 82, 86) stitches.

Starting with a knit row, continue in stockinette stitch until the back measures 24½ (24½, 24½, 25¼, 25¼)" (62 [62, 62, 64, 64]cm) from the start of cast-on edge, ending with a wrong-side row.

SHAPE SHOULDERS

Bind off 23 (24, 25, 26, 28) stitches at the beginning of the next 2 rows.

Leave the center 24 (26, 28, 30, 30) stitches on a holder.

LEFT FRONT

With size 10.5 (7mm) needles, cast on 37 (39, 41, 43, 45) stitches.

Starting with a knit row, continue in stockinette stitch until the left front measures 21¼ (21¼, 21¼, 22, 22)" (54 [54, 54, 56, 56]cm) from the cast-on edge, ending with a right-side row.

SHAPE NECK

Next row Work 9 (10, 11, 12, 12) stitches, slip these stitches onto a holder, work to end. 28 (29, 30, 31, 33) stitches.

Decrease 1 stitch at the neck edge of the next and every following row until 23 (24, 25, 26, 28) stitches remain.

Continue without shaping in stockinette stitch until the left front measures 24½ (24½, 24½, 25¼, 25¼)" (62 [62, 62, 64, 64]cm) from the cast-on edge, ending with a wrong-side row. Bind off.

Mark the positions for 6 buttons along the front opening edge, positioning the first one ¾" (2cm) from the cast-on edge, the last one ¾" (2cm) before the start of the neck shaping, and the remaining 4 buttons evenly in between.

RIGHT FRONT

With size 10.5 (7mm) needles, cast on 37 (39, 41, 43, 45) stitches.

Starting with a knit row, continue in stockinette stitch until the right front measures ¾" (2cm) from cast-on edge, ending with a wrong-side row.

1st buttonhole row (right side) K2, bind off 2 stitches, knit to end.

2nd buttonhole row Purl to last 2 stitches, cast on 2 stitches, p2.

Continue in stockinette stitch, working the buttonhole rows as above to correspond with the positions marked on left front, until right front measures 21¼ (21¼, 21¼, 22, 22)" (54 [54, 54, 56, 56]cm) from the cast-on edge, ending with a wrong-side row.

Complete as for Left Front from Shape Neck, continuing to work

the buttonhole rows to correspond with the positions marked on left front.

SLEEVES (MAKE TWO)

With size 10.5 (7mm) needles, cast on 40 (40, 40, 44, 44) stitches.

Starting with a knit row, continue in stockinette stitch until the sleeve measures 2" (5cm) from the cast-on edge, ending with a wrong-side row.

Increase 1 stitch at each end of the next row. Continue increasing 1 stitch at each end every 6th row until there are 56 (56, 56, 60, 60) stitches.

Continue without shaping in stockinette stitch until the sleeve measures 17¾" (45cm) from the cast-on edge, ending with a wrong-side row.

Bind off.

LEFT EDGING

Join the shoulder seams. With right side facing and size 10 (6mm) needles, pick up and k104 stitches down the left front opening edge.

Bind off.

RIGHT EDGING

With right side facing and size 10 (6mm) needles, pick up and knit 104 stitches up the right front opening edge.

Bind off.

NECK EDGING

With right side facing and size 10 (6mm) needles, k9 (10, 11, 12, 12) stitches from the holder at the right front, pick up and k13 (13, 13, 15, 15) stitches up the right front neck, k24 (26, 28, 30, 30) stitches from the holder at the center back, pick up and k13 (13, 13, 15, 15) stitches down the left front neck, k9 (10, 11, 12, 12) stitches from the holder at the left front—68 (72, 76, 84, 84) stitches.

Bind off.

FINISHING

Sew on the sleeves, placing the center of the sleeves to the shoulder seams. Join the side and sleeve seams. Position and sew the buttons in place.

bobble cardigan

Featuring an allover bobble pattern, this sumptuous cardigan shows a commitment to texture. Ribbing along the neckline, cuffs, and hem offers handsome detailing. What you have is a charming design in eye-popping berry tones that's as fun to knit as it is to wear.

YARN TYPES

YARN
8 (9, 9, 10, 10) balls of Noro Iro, 75% wool/25% silk, 3½ oz (100g), each approximately 131 yds (123m), shade 9 ⑤ chunky

9 buttons size 1¼" (3cm)

NEEDLES
One pair size 10.5 (7mm) knitting needles or size needed to obtain gauge
One pair size 10 (6mm) knitting needles

GAUGE
12 stitches and 18 rows to 4" (10cm) square over pattern using size 10.5 (7mm) needles.

MEASUREMENTS

to fit chest

32–34	36–38	40–42	44–46	48–50 inches
81–86	91.5–96.5	101.5–106.5	111.5–117	122–127cm

actual measurement

45¼	48¾	50½	53	55¾ inches
115	121.5	128.5	135	141.5cm

length

22	22	22	22¾	22¾ inches
56	56	56	58	58 cm

sleeve length

17¾	17¾	17¾	17¾	17¾ inches
45	45	45	45	45cm

2

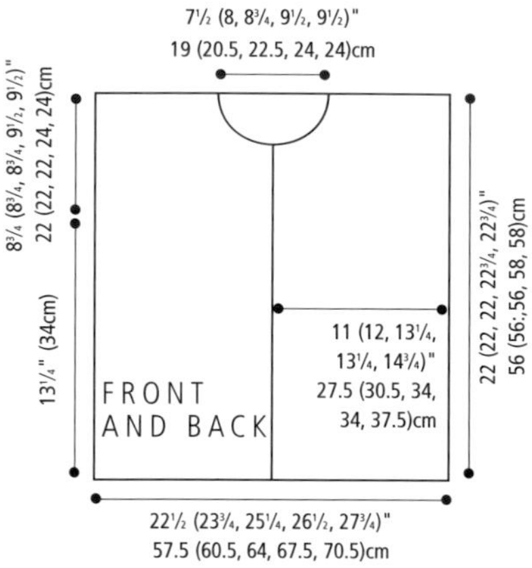
7½ (8, 8¾, 9½, 9½)"
19 (20.5, 22.5, 24, 24)cm
8¾ (8¾, 8¾, 9½, 9½)"
22 (22, 22, 24, 24)cm
13¼" (34cm)
FRONT
AND BACK
11 (12, 13¼, 13¼, 14¾)"
27.5 (30.5, 34, 34, 37.5)cm
22 (22, 22, 22¾, 22¾)"
56 (56, 56, 58, 58)cm
22½ (23¾, 25¼, 26½, 27¾)"
57.5 (60.5, 64, 67.5, 70.5)cm

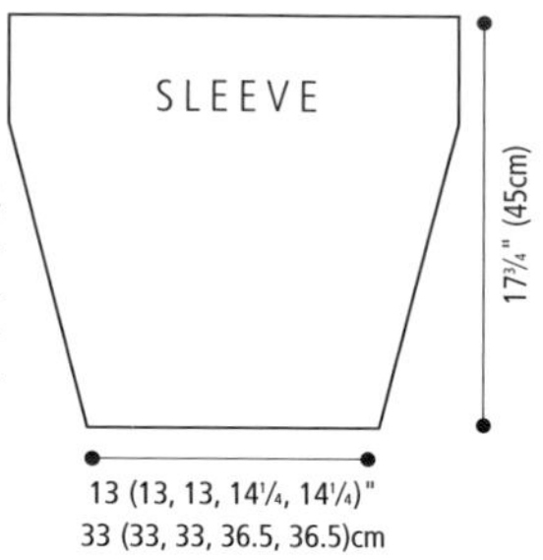
SLEEVE
17¾" (45cm)
13 (13, 13, 14¼, 14¼)"
33 (33, 33, 36.5, 36.5)cm

BACK

With size 10.5 (7mm) needles, cast on 70 (74, 78, 82, 86) stitches.

1st rib row (right side) K2, [p2, k2] to end.

2nd rib row P2, [k2, p2] to end.

These 2 rows form the rib pattern.

Repeat the last 2 rows until the back measures 4¾" (12cm) from the cast-on edge, ending with a right-side row.

Decrease 1 stitch in the middle of the next knit row—69 (73, 77, 81, 85) stitches.

1st pattern row (right side) *P3, [k1 in front, yo, k1 in back] into next stitch; repeat from * to last stitch, p1.

2nd pattern row K1, [p3, k3] to end.

3rd pattern row [P3, k3]to last st, p1.

4th pattern row K1, [p3tog, k3] to end.

5th pattern row Purl to end.

6th pattern row Knit to end.

7th pattern row *P1, [k1 in front, yo, k1 in back] into next stitch, p2; repeat from * to last stitch, p1.

8th pattern row [K3, p3] to last stitch, k1.

9th pattern row P1, [k3, p3] to end.

10th pattern row [K3, p3tog] to last stitch, k1.

11th pattern row Purl to end.

12th pattern row Knit to end.

These 12 rows form the bobble pattern.

Repeat the last 12 rows until the back measures 22 (22, 22, 22¾, 22¾)" (56 [56, 56, 58, 58]cm) from the cast-on edge, ending with a wrong-side row.

SHAPE SHOULDERS

Bind off 23 (24, 25, 26, 28) stitches at the beginning of the next 2 rows.

Leave the center 23 (25, 27, 29, 29) stitches on a holder.

LEFT FRONT

With size 10.5 (7mm) needles, cast on 33 (37, 41, 41, 45) stitches.

1st rib row (right side) [P2, k2] to last stitch, k1.

2nd rib row P1, [p2, k2] to end.

These 2 rows form the rib pattern.

Repeat the last 2 rows until the left front measures 4¾" (12cm) from the cast-on edge, ending with a right-side row.

Knit 1 row.

Starting with a 1st pattern row as given for the Back, continue in bobble pattern until the left front measures 19 (19, 19,19½, 19½)" (48 [48, 48, 50, 50] cm) from the cast-on edge, ending with a right-side row.

SHAPE NECK

Next row Work in pattern 5 (8, 11, 10, 12) stitches, slip these stitches onto a holder, work in pattern to end—28 (29, 30, 31, 33) stitches.

Decrease 1 stitch at the neck edge of the next and every following row until 23 (24, 25, 26, 28) stitches remain.

Continue without shaping in bobble pattern until the left front measures 22 (22, 22, 22¾, 22¾)" (56 [56, 56, 58, 58]cm) from the cast-on edge, ending with a wrong-side row.

Bind off.

RIGHT FRONT

With size 10.5 (7mm) needles, cast on 33 (33, 37, 37, 41) stitches.

1st pattern row (right side) K1, [k2, p2] to end.

2nd pattern row [K2, p2] to last stitch, p1.

These 2 rows form the rib pattern.

Repeat the last 2 rows until the right front measures 4¾" (12cm) from the cast-on edge, ending with a right-side row.

Knit one row.

1st pattern row (right side) *P1, [k1 in front, yo, k1 in back] into next stitch, p2, rep from * to last stitch, p1.

2nd pattern row [K3, p3] to last stitch, k1.

3rd pattern row P1, [k3, p3] to end.

4th pattern row [K3, p3tog] to last stitch, k1.

5th pattern row Purl to end.

6th pattern row Knit to end.

7th pattern row *P3, [k1 in front, yo, k1 in back] into next stitch, repeat from * to last stitch, p1.

8th pattern row K1, [p3, k3] to end.

9th pattern row [P3, k3] to last stitch, p1.

10th pattern row K1, [p3tog, k3] to end.

11th pattern row Purl to end.

12th pattern row Knit to end.

These 12 rows form the bobble pattern.

Repeat the last 12 rows until the right front measures 19 (19,

19, 19¾, 19¾)" (48 [48, 48, 50, 50]cm) from the cast-on edge, ending with a wrong-side row.
Complete as for Left Front from Shape Neck.

SLEEVES (MAKE TWO)

With size 10.5 (7mm) needles, cast on 42 (42, 42, 46, 46) stitches.
Starting with a 1st rib row as given for the Back, continue in rib pattern until the sleeve measures 4" (10cm) from the cast-on edge, ending with a right-side row.
Decrease 1 stitch in the middle of the next knit row—41 (41, 41, 45, 45) stitches.
Starting with a 1st pattern row as given for the Back, continue in bobble pattern, increasing 1 stitch at each end of the next row. Continue increasing 1 stitch at each end every 4th row until there are 57 (57, 57, 61, 61) stitches.
Continue without shaping in bobble pattern until the sleeve measures 17¾" (45cm) from the cast-on edge, ending with a wrong-side row.
Bind off.

LEFT BUTTONBAND EDGING

Join the shoulder seams. With right side facing and size 10 (6mm) needles, pick up and k87 (87, 87, 91, 91) stitches down the left front opening edge.
1st rib row (wrong side) [P2, k2]to last 3 stitches, p3.
2nd rib row K3, [p2, k2] to end.
Repeat the last 2 rows twice more.
Repeat the 1st rib row once more.
Bind off.

RIGHT BUTTONHOLE EDGING

With right side facing and size 10 (6mm) needles, pick up and k87 (87, 87, 91, 91) stitches up the right front opening edge.
1st rib row (wrong side) P3, [k2, p2] to end.
2nd rib row [K2, p2] to last 3 stitches, k3.
Work 1st rib row again.
1st buttonhole row K2, bind off 2 stitches, continue in rib pattern until there are 6 (6, 6, 10, 10) stitches on the right needle after the bind off, *bind off 2 stitches, continue in rib pattern until there are 10 stitches on the right needle after the bind off, repeat from * to last 5 stitches, bind off 2 stitches, work in rib to end.
2nd buttonhole row Work in rib for 3 stitches, *cast on 2 stitches, work in rib for 10 stitches, repeat from * to last 8 (8, 8, 12, 12) stitches, cast on 2 stitches, work in rib for 6 (6, 6, 10, 10), cast on 2 stitches, work in rib for 2 stitches.
Work 2 more rows in rib pattern.
Bind off.

NECK EDGING

With right side facing and size 10 (6mm) needles, pick up and k6 stitches from the buttonhole edging, k5 (8, 11, 10, 12) stitches from the holder at the right front, pick up and k12 (12, 12, 14, 14) stitches up the right front neck, k23 (25, 27, 29, 29) stitches from the holder at the center back increasing 1 stitch at the center, pick up and k12 (12, 12, 14, 14) stitches down the left front neck, k5 (8, 11, 10, 12) stitches from the holder at the left front, pick up and k6 stitches from the buttonband edging—70 (78, 86, 90, 90) stitches.
1st rib row (wrong side) P2, [k2, p2] to end.
2nd rib row K2, [p2, k2] to end.
Work 1st rib row again.
1st buttonhole row K2, bind off 2 stitches, work in rib to end.
2nd buttonhole row [P2, k2] to last 2 stitches, cast on 2 stitches, p2.
Work in rib for 2 rows.
Bind off.

FINISHING

Sew on the sleeves, placing the center of the sleeves against the shoulder seams. Join the side and sleeve seams. Position and sew the buttons in place.

long cardigan

3

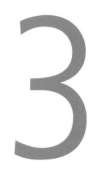

Working with hand-painted yarns is the ultimate indulgence. In a prism of ultracool blue and purple hues, this cool and cozy garter-stitched cardigan is here to stay. The attached scarf is knit with two strands of yarn—Iro and Silk Garden—held together.

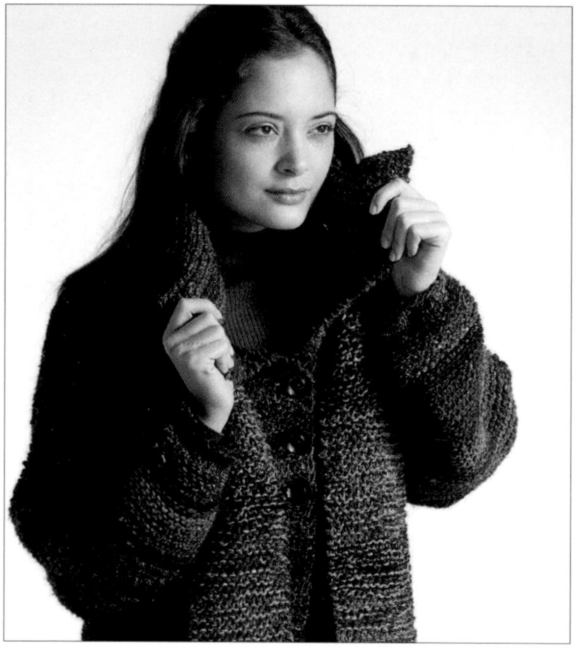

YARN TYPES

YARN

10 (11, 11, 12, 12) balls of Noro Iro, 75% wool/25% silk, 3½ oz (100g), each approximately 131 yds (123m), shade 43 (5) chunky

Two balls of Noro Cash Iroha, 40% silk/30% lambswool/20% cashmere/10% nylon, 1½ oz (40g), each approximately 100 yds (91.5m), shade 92 (5) chunky

The scarf is knitted with one strand of Noro Iro and one strand of Noro Cash Iroha used together throughout.

5 buttons size 1¼" (3cm)

NEEDLES

One pair size 11 (8mm) knitting needles

One pair size 10.5 (7mm) knitting needles or size needed to obtain gauge

One pair size 10 (6mm) knitting needles

GAUGE

12 stitches and 18 rows to 4" (10cm) square over pattern using size 10.5 (7mm) needles.

MEASUREMENTS

to fit chest

32–34	36–38	40–42	44–46	48–50 inches
81–86	91.5–96.5	101.5–106.5	111.5–117	122–127cm

actual measurement

45¾	48½	51	53¾	53¼ inches
116.5	123.5	130	136.5	143.5cm

length

30¾	30¾	30¾	31½	31½ inches
78	78	78	80	80cm

sleeve length

17¾	17¾	17¾	17¾	17¾ inches
45	45	45	45	45cm

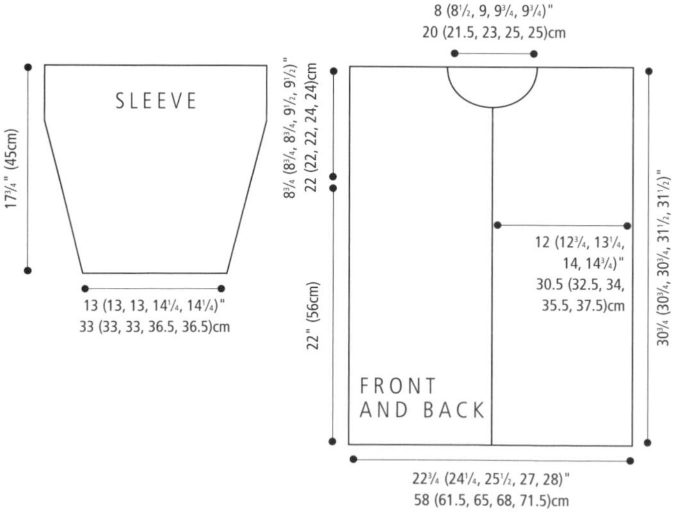

SLEEVE
17¾" (45cm)
13 (13, 13, 14¼, 14¼)"
33 (33, 33, 36.5, 36.5)cm
8 (8½, 9, 9¾, 9¾)"
20 (21.5, 23, 25, 25)cm
8¾ (8¾, 8¾, 9½, 9½)"
22 (22, 22, 24, 24)cm
22" (56cm)
12 (12¾, 13¼, 14, 14¾)"
30.5 (32.5, 34, 35.5, 37.5)cm
30¾ (30¾, 30¾, 31½, 31½)"
78 (78, 78, 80, 80)cm
FRONT AND BACK
22¾ (24¼, 25½, 27, 28)"
58 (61.5, 65, 68, 71.5)cm

BACK

With size 10.5 (7mm) needles, cast on 70 (74, 78, 82, 86) stitches.

Starting with a knit row, work 6 rows in stockinette stitch.
Starting with a knit row, continue in garter stitch until the back measures 30¾ (30¾, 30¾, 31½, 31½)" (78 [78, 78, 80, 80]cm) from the cast-on edge, ending with a wrong-side row.

SHAPE SHOULDERS

Bind off 23 (24, 25, 26, 28) stitches at the beginning of the next 2 rows.
Leave the center 24 (26, 28, 30, 30) stitches on a holder.

LEFT FRONT

With size 10.5 (7mm) needles, cast on 37 (39, 41, 43, 45) stitches.

Starting with a knit row, work 6 rows in stockinette stitch.
Starting with a knit row, continue in garter stitch until the left front measures 27½ (27½, 27½, 28¼, 28¼)" (70 [70, 70, 72, 72]cm) from the cast-on edge, ending with a right-side row.

SHAPE NECK

Next row K9 (10, 11, 12, 12) stitches, slip these stitches onto a holder, knit to end—28 (29, 30, 31, 33) stitches.
Decrease 1 stitch at the neck edge of the next and every following row until 23 (24, 25, 26, 28) stitches remain.
Continue without shaping in garter stitch until the left front measures 30¾ (30¾, 30¾, 31½, 31½)" (78 [78, 78, 80, 80]cm) from the cast-on edge, ending with a wrong-side row.
Bind off.
Mark the positions for 5 buttons along the front opening edge, positioning the first one 21½" (55cm) from the cast-on edge and the last one ¾" (2cm) before the start of the neck shaping, and the remaining buttons in between.

RIGHT FRONT

With size 10.5 (7mm) needles, cast on 37 (39, 41, 43, 45) stitches.

Starting with a knit row, work 6 rows in stockinette stitch.
Starting with a knit row, continue in garter stitch until the right front measures 21½" (55cm) from the cast-on edge, ending with a wrong-side row.
1st buttonhole row (right side) K2, bind off 2 stitches, knit to end.
2nd buttonhole row Knit to last 2 stitches, cast on 2 stitches, k2.
Continue in garter stitch and working the buttonhole rows as above to correspond with the positions marked on left front, until the right front measures 27½ (27½, 27½, 28¼, 28¼)" (70 [70, 70, 72, 72]cm) from the cast-on edge, ending with a

wrong-side row.
Complete as for Left Front from Shape Neck.

SLEEVES (MAKE TWO)

With size 10.5 (7mm) needles, cast on 40 (40, 40, 44, 44) stitches.

Starting with a knit row, work 6 rows in stockinette stitch.
Complete as for Basic Chunky Cardigan Sleeves (page 39), working in garter stitch throughout.

COLLAR

Join the shoulder seams. With right side facing and size 10 (6mm) needles, k9 (10, 11, 12, 12) stitches from the holder at the right front, pick up and k15 (15, 15, 17, 17) stitches up the right neck, k24 (26, 28, 30, 30) stitches from the holder at the center back, pick up and k15 (15, 15, 17, 17) stitches down the left front neck, k9 (10, 11, 12, 12) stitches from the holder at the left front—72 (76, 80, 88, 88) stitches.
Knit 3 rows.
1st buttonhole row K2, bind off 2 stitches, knit to end.
2nd buttonhole row Knit to last 2 stitches, cast on 2 stitches, k2.
Knit 10 rows.
Repeat the 2 buttonhole rows.
Continue in garter stitch until collar measures 4¾" (12cm), ending in a wrong-side row.
Bind off loosely.

Scarf

With size 11 (8mm) needles and one strand of Iro and one strand of Cash Iroha held together, cast on 15 stitches.
Starting with a knit row, continue in garter stitch until work measures 34¾" (88cm) from cast-on edge, ending with a wrong-side row.
Cast off.

FINISHING

Sew on the sleeves, placing the center of the sleeves against the shoulder seams. Join the side and sleeve seams. Position and sew the buttons in place. Sew on scarf to center back neck.

chevron cardigan

4

This mid-length cardigan makes the ideal cover-up for lazy Sunday afternoons. Boasting a textured chevron pattern along the bodice and sleeves, it's a beautiful design that anyone will enjoy.

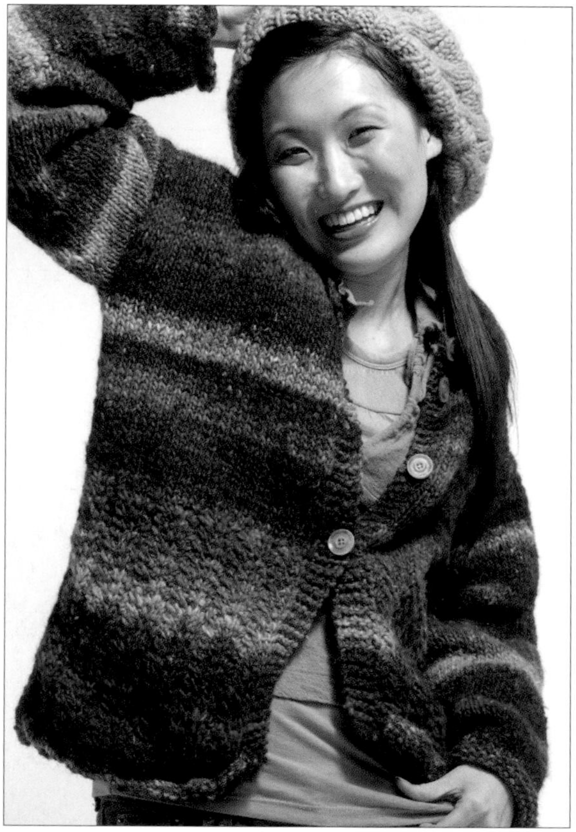

YARN TYPES

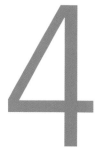

YARN

7 (8, 8, 9, 9) balls of Noro Iro, 75% wool/25% silk, 3½ oz (100g), each approximately 131 yds (123m), shade 72 (5) chunky

NEEDLES

One pair size 10.5 (7mm) knitting needles or size needed to obtain gauge

One pair size 10 (6mm) knitting needles

GAUGE

12 stitches and 18 rows to 4" (10cm) square over stockinette stitch using size 10.5 (7mm) needles.

MEASUREMENTS

to fit chest

32–34	36–38	40–42	44–46	48–50 inches
81–86	91.5–96.5	101.5–106.5	111.5–117	122–127cm

actual measurement

45¾	48½	51	53¾	56½ inches
116.5	123.5	130	136.5	143.5cm

length

24½	24½	24½	25¼	25¼ inches
62	62	62	64	64cm

sleeve length

17¾	17¾	17¾	17¾	17¾ inches
45	45	45	45	45cm

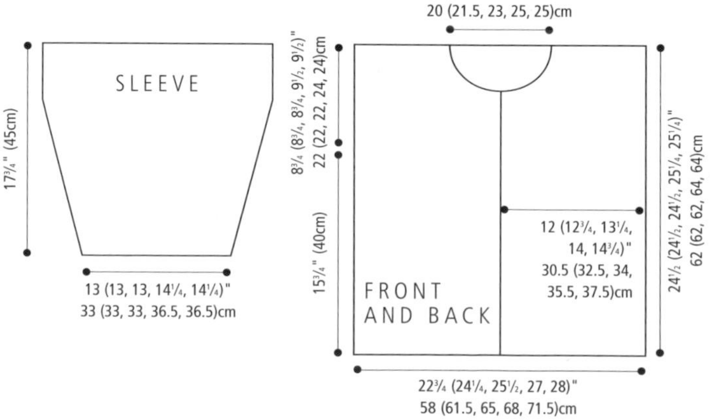

SLEEVE
17¾" (45cm)
13 (13, 13, 14¼, 14¼)"
33 (33, 33, 36.5, 36.5)cm
8 (8½, 9, 9¾, 9¾)"
20 (21.5, 23, 25, 25)cm
8¾ (8¾, 8¾, 9½, 9½)"
22 (22, 22, 24, 24)cm
15¾" (40cm)
12 (12¾, 13¼, 14, 14¾)"
30.5 (32.5, 34, 35.5, 37.5)cm
24½ (24½, 24½, 25¼, 25¼)"
62 (62, 62, 64, 64)cm
FRONT AND BACK
22¾ (24¼, 25½, 27, 28)"
58 (61.5, 65, 68, 71.5)cm

BACK

With size 10.5 (7mm) needles, cast on 83 (88, 94, 98, 104) stitches.

1st pattern row (right side) K3 (2, 2, 1, 1), [m1 by knitting into the front and back of next stitch, k1, sl, k2tog, psso, m1] to last 2 (2, 2, 1, 1) stitch(es), k2 (2, 2, 1, 1).

2nd pattern row Purl.

These 2 rows form the chevron pattern.

Repeat the last 2 rows until the back measures 11" (28cm) from the cast-on edge, ending with a right-side row.

Decrease row P2tog 0 (0, 1, 0, 1) times, p6 (5, 3, 4, 1), p2tog, [p4, p2tog] to last 3 (3, 3, 2, 3) stitches, p3 (3, 1, 2, 1), [p2tog] 0 (0, 1, 0, 1) times—70 (74, 78, 82, 86) stitches.

Starting with a knit row, continue in stockinette stitch until the back measures 24½ (24½, 24½, 25¼, 25¼)" (62 [62, 62, 64, 64]cm) from the start of the cast-on edge, ending with a wrong-side row.

SHAPE SHOULDERS

Bind off 23 (24, 25, 26, 20) stitches at the beginning of the next 2 rows.

Leave the center 24 (26, 28, 30, 30) stitches on a holder.

LEFT FRONT

With size 10.5 (7mm) needles, cast on 43 (45, 48, 50, 53) stitches.

1st pattern row (right side) K2 (3, 2, 2, 1), [m1 by knitting into the front and back of next stitch, k1, sl, k2tog, psso, m1] to last 5 (6, 4, 6, 4) stitches, knit to end.

2nd pattern row K5 (6, 4, 6, 4), purl to end.

These 2 rows form the chevron pattern.

Repeat the last 2 rows until the left front measures 11" (28cm) from the cast-on edge, ending with a right-side row.

Decrease row K5 (6, 4, 6, 4), [p3, p2tog, p1] to last 2 (3, 2, 2, 1) stitch(es), p2 (3, 2, 2, 1)—37 (39, 41, 43, 45) stitches.

Starting with a knit row, continue in stockinette stitch until the left front measures 21¼ (21¼, 21¼, 22, 22)" (54 [54, 54, 56, 56]cm) from the cast-on edge, ending with a right-side row.

SHAPE NECK

Complete as for Basic Chunky Cardigan Left Front from Shape Neck (page 39).

Mark the positions for 3 buttons along the front opening edge, positioning the first one 11¾" (30cm) from the cast-on edge and the last one 1½" (4cm) before the start of the neck shaping, and centering the remaining button in between.

RIGHT FRONT

With size 10.5 (7mm) needles, cast on 43 (45, 48, 50, 53) stitches.

1st pattern row (right side) K5 (6, 4, 6, 4), [m1 by knitting into the front and back of next st, k1, sl, k2tog, psso, m1] to last 2 (3, 2, 2,1) stitches, knit to end.

2nd pattern row Purl to last 5 (6, 4, 6, 4) stitches, knit to end.

These 2 rows form the chevron pattern.

Repeat the last 2 rows until the right front measures 11" (28cm) from the cast-on edge, ending with a right-side row.

Decrease row P2 (3, 2, 2, 1), [p3, p2tog, p1] to last 5 (6, 4, 6, 4) stitches, k5 (6, 4, 6, 4)—37 (39, 41, 43, 45) stitches

1st buttonhole row (right side) K2, bind off 2 stitches, knit to end.

2nd buttonhole row Purl to last 2 stitches, cast on 2 stitches, k2.

Starting with a knit row, continue in stockinette stitch and working the buttonhole rows as above to correspond with the positions marked on the left front until the right front measures 21¼ (21¼, 21¼, 22, 22)" (54 [54, 54, 56, 56]cm) from the cast-on edge, ending with a wrong-side row.

Complete as for Basic Chunky Cardigan Left Front from Shape Neck (page 39).

SLEEVES (MAKE TWO)

Work as for Basic Chunky Cardigan Sleeves (page 39).

COLLAR

With right side facing and size 10 (6mm) needles, k9 (10, 11, 12, 12) stitches from the holder at the right front, pick up and k13 (13, 13, 15, 15) stitches up the right front neck, k24 (26, 28, 30, 30) stitches from the holder at the center back, pick up and k13 (13, 13, 15, 15) stitches down the left front neck, k9 (10, 11, 12, 12) stitches from the holder at the left front—68 (72, 76, 84, 84) stitches.

Knit 3 rows.

1st buttonhole row (right side): K2, bind off 2 stitches, knit to end.

2nd buttonhole row: Knit to last 2 stitches, cast on 2 stitches, k2.

Bind off loosely.

FINISHING

Sew on the sleeves, placing the center of the sleeves against the shoulder seams. Join the side and sleeve seams. Position and sew the buttons in place.

5 ribbed cardigan

A rich spectrum of browns and a handsome allover rib team up in this wonderfully warm and cozy mock turtleneck cardigan that's sure to be an autumn staple. It's been created with a standard zipper, but for a more flexible design, you can sew in a two-way zipper.

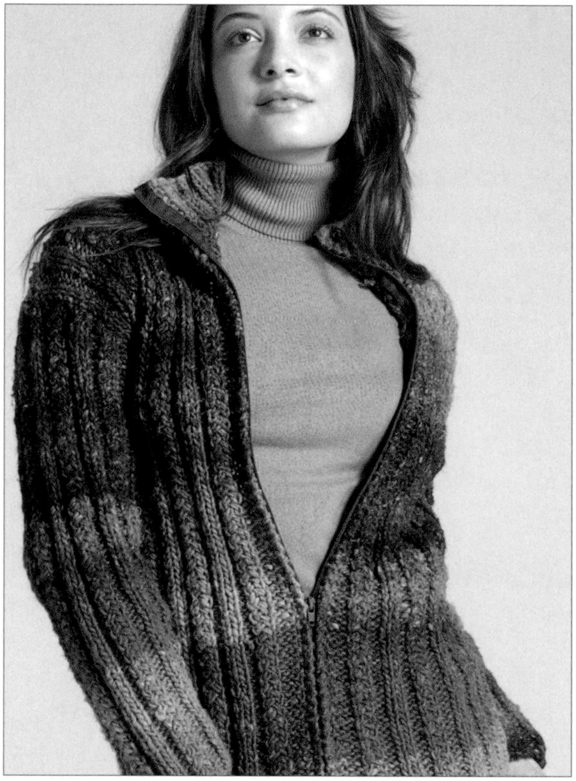

YARN TYPES

YARN

7 (8, 8, 9, 9) balls of Noro Iro, 75% wool/25% silk, 3½ oz (100g), each approximately 131 yds (123m), shade 47 (5) chunky

Open-ended zipper to fit:
First 3 sizes: length 28" (71cm)
Last 2 sizes: length 30" (76cm)

NEEDLES

One pair size 10.5 (7mm) knitting needles or size needed to obtain gauge
One pair size 10 (6mm) knitting needles or size needed to obtain gauge

GAUGE

12 stitches and 18 rows to 4" (10cm) square over pattern when stretched using size 10.5 (7mm) needles.

MEASUREMENTS

to fit chest

32–34	36–38	40–42	44–46	48–50 inches
81–86	91.5–96.5	101.5–106.5	111.5–117	122–127cm

actual measurement

45¾	48½	51	53¾	56½ inches
116.5	123.5	130	136.5	143.5cm

length

24½	24½	24½	25¼	25¼ inches
62	62	62	64	64cm

sleeve length

17¾	17¾	17¾	17¾	17¾ inches
45	45	45	45	45cm

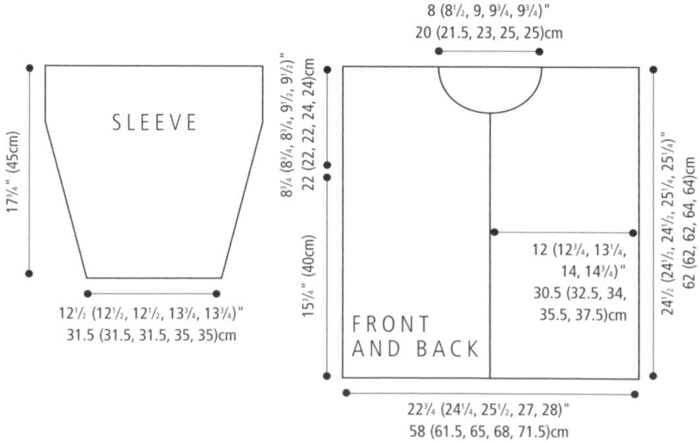

SLEEVE
17¾" (45cm)
12½ (12½, 12½, 13¾, 13¾)"
31.5 (31.5, 31.5, 35, 35)cm
8 (8½, 9, 9¾, 9¾)"
20 (21.5, 23, 25, 25)cm
8¾ (8¾, 8¾, 9½, 9½)"
22 (22, 22, 24, 24)cm
15¾" (40cm)
12 (12¾, 13¼,
14, 14¾)"
30.5 (32.5, 34,
35.5, 37.5)cm
24½ (24½, 24½, 25¼, 25¼)"
62 (62, 62, 64, 64)cm
FRONT
AND BACK
22¾ (24¼, 25½, 27, 28)"
58 (61.5, 65, 68, 71.5)cm

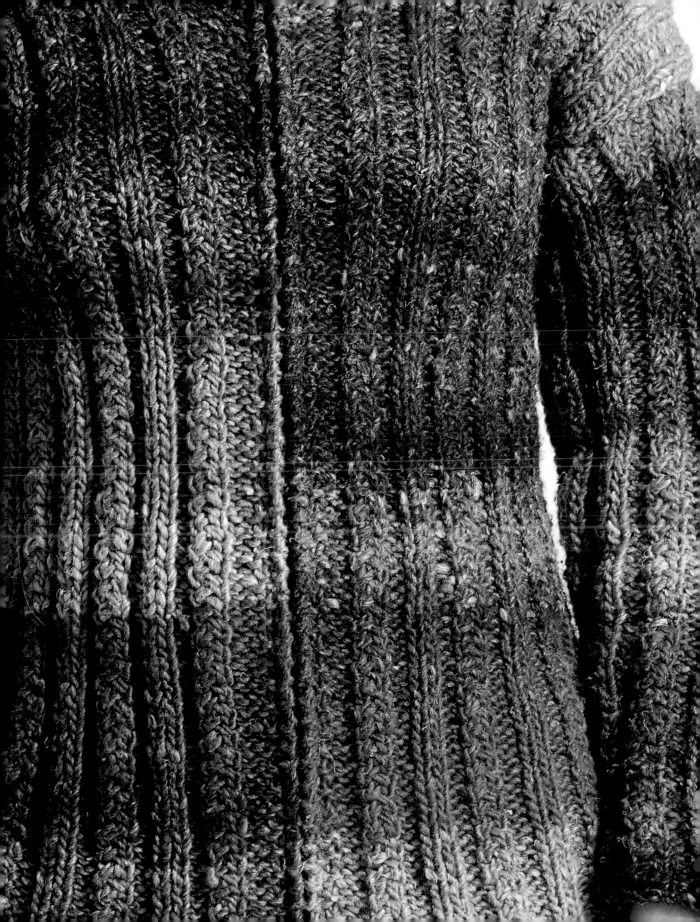

BACK

With size 10.5 (7mm) needles, cast on 70 (74, 78, 82, 86) stitches.

1st rib row (right side) K3 (2, 2,1, 1), p2 (0, 2, 0, 2), k2 (0, 2, 0, 2), [p2, T2K, k1, p2, k2] to end.

2nd rib row [P2, k2, T2P, p1, k2] to last 7 (2, 6, 1, 5) stitches, p2 (0, 2, 0, 2), k2 (0, 2, 0,), p3 (2, 2, 1, 1).

These 2 rows form the rib pattern.

Repeat the last 2 rows until the back measures 24½ (24½, 24½, 25¼, 25¼)" (62 [62, 62, 64, 64]cm) from the cast-on edge, ending with a wrong-side row.

SHAPE SHOULDERS

Bind off 23 (24, 25, 26, 28) stitches at the beginning of the next 2 rows.

Leave the center 24 (26, 28, 30, 30) stitches on a holder.

LEFT FRONT

With size 10.5 (7mm) needles, cast on 35 (37, 39, 41, 43) stitches.

1st rib row (right side) P1 (3, 0, 0, 0), k2 (2, 0, 0, 2), p2 (2, 0, 2, 2), [k2, p2, T2K, k1, p2] to last 3 stitches, k3.

2nd rib row K3, [k2, T2P, p1, k2, p2] to last 5 (7, 0, 2, 4) stitches, k2 (2, 0, 2, 2), p2 (2, 0, 0, 2), k1(3, 0, 0, 0).

These 2 rows form the rib pattern with the edge 3 stitches as garter stitch.

Repeat the last 2 rows until the left front measures 21¼ (21¼, 21¼, 22, 22)" (54 [54, 54, 56, 56]cm) from the cast-on edge, ending with a right-side row.

SHAPE NECK

Next row Work 7 (8, 9, 10, 10) stitches in pattern, slip these stitches onto a holder, work in pattern to end—28 (29, 30, 31, 33) stitches.

Decrease 1 stitch at the neck edge of the next and every following row until 23 (24, 25, 26, 28) stitches remain. Continue without shaping in rib pattern until the left front measures 24½ (24½, 24½, 25¼, 25¼)" (62 [62, 62, 64, 64]cm) from the cast-on edge, ending with a wrong-side row. Bind off.

RIGHT FRONT

With size 10.5 (7mm) needles, cast on 35 (37, 39, 41, 43) stitches.

1st rib row (right side) K3, [p2, T2K, k1, p2, k2] to last 5 (7, 0, 2, 4) stitches, p2 (2, 0, 2, 2), k2 (2, 0, 0, 2), p1 (3, 0, 0, 0).

2nd rib row K1 (3, 0, 0, 0), p2 (2, 0, 0, 2), k2 (2, 0, 2, 2), [p2, k2, T2P, p1, k2] to last 3 stitches, knit to end.

These 2 rows form the rib pattern with the 3 edge stitches in garter stitch.

Repeat the last 2 rows until the right front measures 21¼ (21¼, 21¼, 22, 22)" (54 [54, 54, 56, 56]cm) from the cast-on edge, ending with a wrong-side row.

Complete as for left front from Shape Neck.

SLEEVES (MAKE TWO)

With size 10.5 (7mm) needles, cast on 38 (38, 38, 42, 42) stitches.

1st rib row (right side) K2, p0 (0, 0, 2, 2), k0 (0, 0, 2, 2), [p2, T2K, k1, p2, k2] to end.

2nd rib row [P2, k2, T2P, p1, k2] to last 2 (2, 2, 6, 6) stitches, p0 (0, 0, 2, 2), k0 (0, 0, 2, 2), p2.

These 2 rows form the rib pattern.

Repeat the last 2 rows until the sleeve measures 2" (5cm) from the cast-on edge, ending with a wrong-side row.

Continue in rib pattern, increasing 1 stitch at each end of the next row and then every 4th row until there are 54 (54, 54, 60, 60) stitches.

Continue without shaping in rib pattern until the sleeve measures 17¾" (45cm) from the cast-on edge, ending with a wrong-side row.

Bind off.

COLLAR

Join the shoulder seams. With right side facing and size 10 (6mm) needles, k7 (8, 9, 10, 10) stitches from the holder at the right front, pick up and k13 (13, 13, 15, 15) stitches up the right neck, k24 (26, 28, 30, 30) stitches from the holder at the center back, pick up and k13 (13, 13, 15, 15) stitches down the left front neck, k7 (8, 9, 10, 10) stitches from the holder at the left front—64 (68, 72, 80, 80) stitches.

1st rib row (wrong side) K5, p2, [k2, p2]to last 5 stitches, knit to end.

2nd rib row K3, p2, [k2, p2] to last 3 stitches, k3.

Repeat the last 2 rows until the collar measures 4¾" (12cm), ending with a wrong-side row.

Bind off.

FINISHING

Sew on the sleeves, placing the center of the sleeves against the shoulder seams. Join the side and sleeve seams. Position and sew the zipper in place.

PULLOVERS

basic pullover

Unite style with function with this basic pullover design. Knit in easy stockinette and without any shaping, the basic design offers the creative freedom to play up the design and make a truly custom-made garment. Rolled hems make a fun detail as well.

YARN TYPES

YARN
7 (7, 8, 8, 9) balls of Noro Kureyon, 100% wool, 1¾ oz (50g), each approximately 110 yds (100m), shade 164 ❹ medium

NEEDLES
One pair size 8 (5mm) knitting needles or size needed to obtain gauge
One pair size 6 (4mm) knitting needles

GAUGE
18 stitches and 24 rows to 4" (10cm) square over stockinette stitch using size 8 (5mm) needles.

MEASUREMENTS
to fit chest

32–34	34–36	36–38	40–42	42–44 inches
81–86	86–91.5	91.5–96.5	101.5–106.5	106.5–111.5cm

actual measurement

35¾	37½	41	43	46¼ inches
91	95.5	104.5	109	117.5cm

length

22	22	22	22¾	22¾ inches
56	56	56	58	58cm

sleeve length

18	18	18	18	18 inches
46	46	46	46	46cm

1

BACK

With size 8 (5mm) needles, cast on 82 (86, 94, 98, 106) stitches.

Starting with a knit row, continue in stockinette stitch until the back measures 13¼" (34cm) from the cast-on edge, ending with a wrong-side row.

SHAPE ARMHOLES

Bind off 4 stitches at the beginning of the next 2 rows—74 (78, 86, 90, 98) stitches.

Decrease 1 stitch at each end of the next row. Then decrease 1 stitch at each end of every 4th row three times—66 (70, 78, 82, 90) stitches.

Continue without shaping in stockinette stitch until the armhole measures 8½ (8½, 8½, 9½, 9½)" (22 [22, 22, 24, 24]cm) from the start of the armhole shaping, ending with a wrong-side row.

SHAPE SHOULDERS

Bind off 18 (20, 23, 25, 28) stitches at the beginning of the next 2 rows.

Leave the remaining 30 (30, 32, 32, 34) stitches on a holder.

FRONT

Work as for the Back until the armhole measures 5½ (5½, 5½, 6¼, 6¼)" (14 [14, 14, 16, 16]cm) from the start of the armhole shaping, ending with a wrong-side row.

SHAPE LEFT NECK

Next row K22 (24, 27, 29, 32), slip the remaining stitches onto a holder, turn.

Decrease one stitch at the neck edge of the next row and then every other row until 18 (20, 23, 25, 28) stitches remain.

Continue without shaping in stockinette stitch until the armhole measures 8½ (8½, 8½, 9½, 9½)" (22 [22, 22, 24, 24]cm) from the start of the armhole shaping, ending with a wrong-side row.

Bind off.

SHAPE RIGHT NECK

With right side facing, leaving the center 22 (22, 24, 24, 26) stitches on holder, rejoin the yarn to the remaining stitches and knit to end.

Decrease 1 stitch at the neck edge of the next row and then every other row until 18 (20, 23, 25, 28) stitches remain.

Continue without shaping in stockinette stitch until the armhole measures 8½ (8½, 8½, 9½, 9½)" (22 [22, 22, 24, 24]cm) from the start of the armhole shaping, ending with a wrong-side row.

Bind off.

SLEEVES (MAKE TWO)

With size 8 (5mm) needles, cast on 54 (54, 54, 62, 62) stitches.

Starting with a knit row, continue in stockinette stitch until the sleeve measures 18" (46cm) from the cast-on edge, ending with a wrong-side row.

SHAPE SLEEVE CAP

Bind off 4 stitches at the beginning of the next 2 rows. 46 (46, 46, 54, 54) stitches.

Work 2 rows in stockinette stitch.

Decrease 1 stitch at each end of the next and the 5 following 4th rows—34 (34, 34, 42, 42) stitches.

Purl 1 row.

Decrease 1 stitch at each end of next and the 2 following alternate rows—28 (28, 28, 36, 36) stitches.

Work 3 (3, 3, 5, 5) rows in stockinette stitch.

Decrease one stitch at each end of the next and every following row until 18 (18, 18, 22, 22) stitches remain.

Bind off 4 stitches at the beginning of the next 2 rows—10 (10, 10, 14, 14) stitches.

Bind off the remaining stitches.

NECK

Join the right shoulder seam. With right side facing and size 6 (4mm) needles, pick up and k20 stitches down the left front neck, k22 (22, 24, 24, 26) stitches from the holder at the center front, pick up and k20 stitches up the right front neck, k30 (30, 32, 32, 34) stitches from the holder at the center back—92 (92, 96, 96, 100) stitches.

Bind off loosely.

FINISHING

Join the left shoulder seam and neck edge. Sew on the sleeves, placing the center of the sleeves against the shoulder seams. Join the side and sleeve seams.

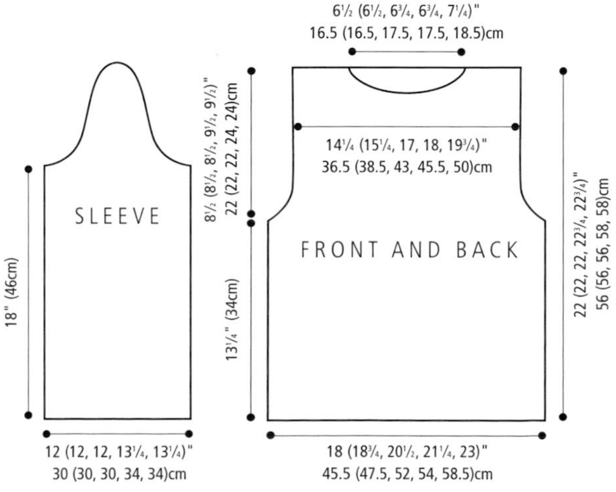

6½ (6½, 6¾, 6¾, 7¼)"
16.5 (16.5, 17.5, 17.5, 18.5)cm
SLEEVE
18" (46cm)
12 (12, 12, 13¼, 13¼)"
30 (30, 30, 34, 34)cm
8½ (8½, 8½, 9½, 9½)"
22 (22, 22, 24, 24)cm
13¼" (34cm)
14¼ (15¼, 17, 18, 19¾)"
36.5 (38.5, 43, 45.5, 50)cm
FRONT AND BACK
22 (22, 22, 22¾, 22¾)"
56 (56, 56, 58, 58)cm
18 (18¾, 20½, 21¼, 23)"
45.5 (47.5, 52, 54, 58.5)cm

v-neck pullover

A plunging V-neck, rolled hems, and cropped ¾-length sleeves work together in this tireless design. For a slightly quirkier look, shorten the sleeves and extend the length. Paired with a wide belt, it's a fresh new take on a classic.

YARN TYPES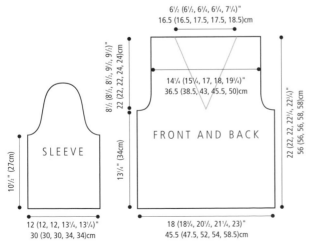

YARN
7 (7, 8, 8, 9) balls of Noro Silk Garden, 45% silk/45% mohair/10% lambswool, 1¾ oz (50g), each approximately 110 yds (100m), shade 86 (4️⃣) medium

NEEDLES
One pair size 8 (5mm) knitting needles or size needed to obtain gauge

GAUGE
18 stitches and 24 rows to 4" (10cm) square over stockinette stitch using size 8 (5mm) needles.

MEASUREMENTS
to fit chest

32–34	34–36	36–38	40–42	42–44 inches
81–86	86–91.5	91.5–96.5	101.5–106.5	106.5–111.5cm

actual measurement

35¾	37½	41	43	46¼ inches
91	95.5	104.5	109	117.5cm

length

22	22	22	22¾	22¾ inches
56	56	56	58	58cm

sleeve length

10½	10½	10½	10½	10½ inches
27	27	27	27	27cm

BACK
Work as for Basic Pullover Back (page 57).

FRONT
Work as for Back to Armhole Shaping.

SHAPE ARMHOLE AND LEFT NECK
Next row Bind off 4 stitches, knit until there are 37 (39, 43, 45, 49) stitches on the right needle, slip the remaining stitches onto a holder, turn.
Purl one row.
Next row Decrease 1 stitch at armhole edge. Then decrease 1 stitch at armhole edge every 4th row three times; **at the same time** decrease 1 stitch at the neck edge of the next and every other row until 18 (20, 23, 25, 28) stitches remain.
Continue without shaping in stockinette stitch until the armhole measures 8½ (8½, 8½, 9½, 9½)" (22 [22, 22, 24, 24]cm) from the start of the armhole shaping, ending with a wrong-side row. Bind off.

SHAPE ARMHOLE AND RIGHT NECK
With right side facing, rejoin the yarn to the remaining stitches, knit to end.
Next row Bind off 4 stitches, purl to end.
Next row Decrease 1 stitch at armhole edge. Then decrease 1 stitch at armhole edge every 4th row three times; **at the same time** decrease 1 stitch at the neck edge of the next and every other row until 18 (20, 23, 25, 28) stitches remain.
Continue without shaping in stockinette stitch until the armhole measures 8½ (8½, 8½, 9½, 9½)" (22 [22, 22, 24, 24]cm) from the start of the armhole shaping, ending with a wrong-side row. Bind off.

SLEEVES (MAKE TWO)
With size 8 (5mm) needles, cast on 54 (54, 54, 62, 62) stitches. Starting with a knit row, continue in garter stitch until the sleeve measures 4¾" (12cm) from the cast-on edge, ending with a wrong-side row.
Starting with a knit row, continue in stockinette stitch until the sleeve measures 10½" (27cm) from the cast-on edge, ending with a wrong-side row.
Work as for Basic Pullover Shape Sleeve Cap (page 57).

FINISHING
Join the shoulder seams. Sew on the sleeves, placing the center of the sleeves against the shoulder seams. Join the side and sleeve seams.

6½ (6½, 6¾, 6¾, 7¼)"
16.5 (16.5, 17.5, 17.5, 18.5)cm

8½ (8½, 8½, 9½, 9½)"
22 (22, 22, 24, 24)cm

14¼ (15¼, 17, 18, 19¼)"
36.5 (38.5, 43, 45.5, 50)cm

FRONT AND BACK

22 (22, 22, 22¾, 22¾)"
56 (56, 56, 58, 58)cm

13¼" (34cm)

SLEEVE

10½" (27cm)

12 (12, 12, 13¼, 13¼)"
30 (30, 30, 34, 34)cm

18 (18¼, 20½, 21¼, 23)"
45.5 (47.5, 52, 54, 58.5)cm

striped pullover

A soft feminine silhouette and dramatic coloring set the tone of this winter warmer. It's been updated with a 2x2 rib along the bodice and sleeves. Pair it with jeans for a casual look or with an A-line skirt for a flirtier option.

3

YARN TYPES

YARN
4 (4, 5, 5, 6) balls of Kureyon, 100% wool, 1¾ oz (50g), each approximately 110 yds (100m), shade 40 (A) **4** medium

4 (4, 5, 5, 6) balls of Kureyon, 100% wool, 1¾ oz (50g), each approximately 110 yds (100m), shade 212 (B) **4** medium

NEEDLES
One pair size 8 (5mm) knitting needles or size needed to obtain gauge

GAUGE
18 stitches and 24 rows to 4" (10cm) square over stockinette stitch using size 8 (5mm) needles.

MEASUREMENTS
to fit chest

32–34	34–36	36–38	40–42	42–44 inches
81–86	86–91.5	91.5–96.5	101.5–106.5	106.5–111.5cm

actual measurement

35¾	37½	41	43	46¼ inches
91	95.5	104.5	109	117.5cm

length

22	22	22	22¾	22¾ inches
56	56	56	58	58cm

sleeve length

10½	10½	10½	10½	10½ inches
27	27	27	27	27cm

12-ROW STRIPED PATTERN

Work 6 rows in B.
Work 6 rows in A.
These 12 rows form the striped pattern; repeat throughout.

BACK

With size 8 (5mm) needles and A, cast on 82 (86, 94, 98, 106) stitches.
1st rib row K2, [p2, k2] to end.
2nd rib row P2, [k2, p2] to end.
These 2 rows form the rib pattern.
Repeat the last 2 rows until the back measures 8½" (22cm) from the cast-on edge, ending with a wrong-side row.
Starting with a knit row and B, continue in stockinette stitch and striped pattern until the back measures 13¼" (34cm) from the cast-on edge, ending with a wrong-side row.

SHAPE ARMHOLES

Complete as for Basic Pullover Front from Shape Armholes (page 57), working in striped pattern throughout.

FRONT

Work as for Basic Pullover Front (page 57), working in stockinette stitch and striped pattern throughout.

SLEEVES (MAKE TWO)

With size 8 (5mm) needles, cast on 54 (54, 54, 62, 62) stitches.
Starting with a 1st rib row, continue in rib pattern until the sleeve measures 2" (5cm) from the cast-on edge, ending with a wrong-side row.
Starting with a knit row and B, continue in stockinette stitch and striped pattern until the sleeve measures 10½" (27cm) from the cast-on edge, ending with a wrong-side row.

SHAPE SLEEVE CAP

Work as for Basic Pullover Shape Sleeve Cap (page 57), working in stockinette stitch and striped pattern throughout.

NECK

Join the right shoulder seam. With right side facing, size 6 (4mm) needles, and B, pick up and k23 stitches down the left front neck, k22 (22, 24, 24, 26) stitches from the holder at the center front, pick up and k23 stitches up the right front neck, k30 (30, 32, 32, 34) stitches from the holder at the center back—98 (98, 102, 102, 106) stitches.
1st rib row K3, [p2, k2] to last 3 stitches, p3.
2nd rib row Work in rib pattern for 22 stitches, k2togtbl, work in rib pattern 20 (20, 22, 22, 24) stitches, k2tog, work in rib pattern to end.
3rd rib row Work in rib pattern for 51 (51, 53, 53, 55) stitches, p2tog, work in rib pattern for 18 (18, 20, 20, 22) stitches, p2togtbl, work in rib pattern to end.
Bind off loosely.

FINISHING

Join the left shoulder seam and neck edge. Sew on the sleeves, placing the center of the sleeves to the shoulder seams. Join the side and sleeve seams.

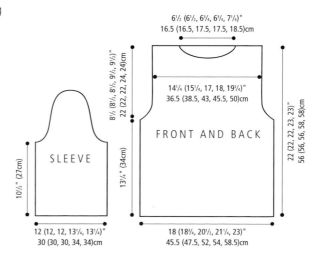

6½ (6½, 6¾, 6¾, 7¼)"
16.5 (16.5, 17.5, 17.5, 18.5)cm

14¼ (15¼, 17, 18, 19¼)"
36.5 (38.5, 43, 45.5, 50)cm

8½ (8½, 8½, 9½, 9½)"
22 (22, 22, 24, 24)cm

FRONT AND BACK

22 (22, 22, 23, 23)"
56 (56, 56, 58, 58)cm

SLEEVE

10½" (27cm)

13¼" (34cm)

12 (12, 12, 13¼, 13¼)"
30 (30, 30, 34, 34)cm

18 (18¾, 20½, 21¼, 23)"
45.5 (47.5, 52, 54, 58.5)cm

tunic/dress

A luxe yarn, dazzling colors, and easy stitches are the basis of a new sophistication in this downtown chic dress. Featuring a relaxed fit, garter-stitched collar, and rolled edges, it can be worn either as a dress or tunic.

4

YARN

6 (7, 7, 8, 8) balls of Noro Silk Garden, 45% silk/45% mohair/10% lambswool, 1¾ oz (50g), each approximately 110 yds (100m), shade 264 (A) **(4)** medium

6 (7, 7, 8, 8) balls of Noro Silk Garden, 45% silk/45% mohair/10% lambswool, 1¾ oz (50g), each approximately 110 yds (100m), shade 226 (B) **(4)** medium

NEEDLES

One pair size 8 (5mm) knitting needles or size needed to obtain gauge

GAUGE

18 stitches and 24 rows to 4" (10cm) square over stockinette stitch using size 8 (5mm) needles.

MEASUREMENTS

to fit chest

32–34	34–36	36–38	40–42	42–44 inches
81–86	86–91.5	91.5–96.5	101.5–106.5	106.5–111.5cm

actual measurement

35¾	37½	41	43	46¼ inches
91	95.5	104.5	109	117.5cm

length

30¼	30¼	30¼	31	31 inches
77	77	77	79	79cm

sleeve length

18	18	18	18	18 inches
46	46	46	46	46cm

STRIPED PATTERN

Work 2 rows in A.
Work 2 rows in B.
These 4 rows form the striped pattern; repeat throughout.

BACK

With size 8 (5mm) needles and A, cast on 82 (86, 94, 98, 106) stitches.
Starting with a knit row, continue in stockinette stitch and striped pattern until the back measures 21½" (55cm) from the cast-on edge, ending with a wrong-side row.

SHAPE ARMHOLES

Complete as for Basic Pullover Back from Shape Armholes (page 57), working in stockinette stitch and striped pattern throughout.

FRONT

Work as for the Back until Shape Armholes, then continue to work as Basic Pullover Front (page 57), working in stockinette stitch and striped pattern throughout.

SLEEVES (MAKE TWO)

Casting on with A, work as for Basic Pullover Sleeves (page 57), working in stockinette stitch and striped pattern throughout.

NECK

Join the right shoulder seam. With right side facing, size 8 (5mm) needles, and A, pick up and k16 stitches down the left front neck, k22 (22, 24, 24, 26) stitches from the holder at the center front, pick up and k16 stitches up the right front neck, k30 (30, 32, 32, 34) stitches from the holder at the center back—84 (84, 88, 88, 92) stitches.
Starting with a knit row, continue in garter stitch until the neck measures 12" (30cm), ending with a wrong-side row.
Bind off loosely.

FINISHING

Join the left shoulder seam and neck edge, reversing the seam halfway along the neck if desired. Sew on the sleeves, placing the center of the sleeves against the shoulder seams. Join the side and sleeve seams.

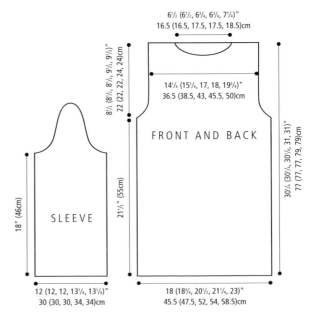

YARN TYPES ▢

YARN

2 (3, 3, 4, 4) balls of Noro Kureyon, 100% wool, 1¾ oz (50g) each approximately 110 yds (100m), shade 164 (A) **(4)** medium

3 (3, 4, 4, 5) balls of Noro Kureyon, 100% wool, 1¾ oz (50g) each approximately 110 yds (100m), shade 154 (B) **(4)** medium

2 (3, 3, 4, 4) balls of Noro Kureyon, 100% wool, 1¾ oz (50g) each approximately 110 yds (100m), shade 213 (C) **(4)** medium

2 (3, 3, 4, 4) balls of Noro Kureyon, 100% wool, 1¾ oz (50g) each approximately 110 yds (100m), shade 182 (D) **(4)** medium

NEEDLES

One pair size 8 (5mm) knitting needles or size needed to obtain gauge
One pair size 6 (4mm) knitting needles

GAUGE

18 stitches and 24 rows to 4" (10cm) square over stockinette stitch using size 8 (5mm) needles.

MEASUREMENTS

to fit chest

32–34	34–36	36–38	40–42	42–44 inches
81–86	86–91.5	91.5–96.5	101.5–106.5	106.5–111.5cm

actual measurement

35¾	37½	41	43	46¼ inches
91	95.5	104.5	109	117.5cm

length

22	22	22	22¾	22¾ inches
56	56	56	58	58cm

sleeve length

10½	10½	10½	10½	10½ inches
27	27	27	27	27cm

chevron pullover

This casual design works best when knit in vibrant colors, and this shade certainly does the trick. A chevron is paired with stripes along the body and sleeves and offers maximum appeal. The ¾-length sleeves have a subtle bell shape to highlight the pattern. For a similar cardigan version, see the Chevron Cardigan on page 108.

5

10-ROW STRIPED PATTERN

Work 2 rows with B.
Work 2 rows with C.
Work 2 rows with D.
Work 2 rows with B.
Work 2 rows with A.
These 10 rows form the striped pattern; repeat throughout.

BACK

With size 8 (5mm) needles and A, cast on 91 (93, 104, 106, 117) stitches.

1st pattern row (right side) K0 (1, 0, 1, 0), [m1 by knitting into the front and back of next stitch, k4, sl, k2tog, psso, k4, m1] to last 0 (1, 0, 1, 0) stitch, knit to end.

2nd pattern row Purl.

These 2 rows form the chevron pattern.

Repeat the last 2 rows and the striped pattern until the back measures 8½" (22cm) from the cast-on edge, ending with a right-side row

First, third, and fifth sizes only

Decrease row P2tog, p4, p2tog, [p11, p2tog] to last 5 stitches, p3, p2tog—82 (–, 94, –, 106) stitches.

Second and fourth sizes only

Decrease row P1, [p6, p2tog, p5] to last stitch, p1— – (86, –, 98, –) stitches.

All sizes

Starting with a knit row, continue in stockinette stitch and striped pattern until the back measures 13¼" (34cm) from the cast-on edge, ending with a wrong-side row.

SHAPE ARMHOLES

Complete as for Basic Pullover from Shape Armholes (page 57), working in stockinette stitch and striped pattern throughout.

FRONT

Work as for the Back until Armhole Shaping. Complete as for V-Neck Pullover from Shape Armhole and Left Neck (page 59), working in stockinette stitch and striped pattern throughout.

SLEEVES (MAKE TWO)

With size 8 (5mm) needles and A, cast on 65 (65, 65, 78, 78) stitches.

1st pattern row (right side) [M1 by knitting into the front and back of next st, k4, sl, k2tog, psso, k4, m1] to end.

2nd pattern row Purl.

These 2 rows form the chevron pattern.

Repeat the last 2 rows and the striped pattern until the sleeve measures 6" (15cm) from the cast-on edge, ending with a right-side row.

First, second, and third sizes only

Decrease row P2tog, p3, s1, p2tog, psso, *p10, s1, p2tog, psso, rep from * to last 5 stitches, p5—54 (54, 54, –, –) stitches

Fourth and fifth sizes only

Decrease row P1, p2tog, [p3, p2tog] 15 times— – (–, –, 62, 62) stitches.

All sizes

Starting with a knit row, continue in stockinette stitch and striped pattern until the sleeve measures 10½" (27cm) from the cast-on edge, ending with a wrong-side row.

SHAPE SLEEVE CAP

Complete as for Basic Pullover from Shape Sleeve Cap (page 57), working in striped pattern throughout.

NECK

Join the right shoulder seam. With right side facing, size 6 (4mm) needles, and A, pick up and k55 stitches down the left front neck, pick up and k55 stitches up the right front neck, k30 (30, 32, 32, 34) stitches from the holder at the center back—140 (140, 142, 142, 144) stitches.

Knit 1 row.

Bind off loosely.

FINISHING

Join the left shoulder seam and neck edge. Sew on the sleeves, placing the center of the sleeves against the shoulder seams. Join the side and sleeve seams.

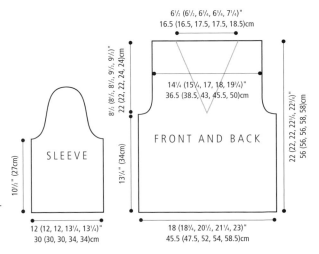

6½ (6½, 6¾, 6¾, 7¼)"
16.5 (16.5, 17.5, 17.5, 18.5)cm

8½ (8½, 8½, 9½, 9½)"
22 (22, 22, 24, 24)cm

14¼ (15¼, 17, 18, 19¼)"
36.5 (38.5, 43, 45.5, 50)cm

22 (22, 22, 22¼, 22¼)"
56 (56, 56, 58, 58)cm

FRONT AND BACK

SLEEVE

10½" (27cm)

13¼" (34cm)

12 (12, 12, 13¼, 13¼)"
30 (30, 30, 34, 34)cm

18 (18¾, 20½, 21¼, 23)"
45.5 (47.5, 52, 54, 58.5)cm

6

ribbed v-neck pullover

The gorgeous striped pattern in Noro Silk Garden gives this figure-skimming ribbed pullover
a unique twist. The deep V-neck design is flattering, and the rib pattern will have a stream-
lining effect on any body shape.

YARN

7 (7, 8, 8, 9) balls of Noro Silk Garden, 45% silk/45% mohair/10% lambswool, 1¾ oz (50g), each approximately 110 yds (100m), shade 87 ④ medium

NEEDLES

One pair size 8 (5mm) knitting needles or size needed to obtain gauge

GAUGE

18 stitches and 24 rows to 4" (10cm) square over rib pattern when slightly stretched using size 8 (5mm) needles.

MEASUREMENTS

to fit chest

32–34	34–36	36–38	40–42	42–44 inches
81 86	86 91.5	91.5–96.5	101.5–106.5	106.5–111.5cm

actual measurement

35¾	37½	40¾	42¾	46¼ inches
91	95.5	104	108.5	117.5cm

length

22	22	22	22¾	22¾ inches
56	56	56	58	58cm

sleeve length

18	18	18	18	18 inches
46	46	46	46	46cm

BACK

With size 8 (5mm) needles, cast on 82 (86, 94, 98,106) stitches.
1st rib row K2, [p2, k2] to end.
2nd rib row P2, [k2, p2] to end.
These 2 rows form the rib pattern.
Repeat the last 2 rows until the back measures 13¼" (34cm) from the cast-on edge, ending with a wrong-side row.

SHAPE ARMHOLES

Complete as for Basic Pullover Back from Shape Armholes (page 57), working in rib pattern throughout.

FRONT

Work as for Back until Shape Armholes.
Continue as for V-Neck Pullover from Shape Armhole and Left Neck (page 59), working in rib pattern throughout and making decreases 4 stitches in from the neck edge.

SLEEVES (MAKE TWO)

Work as for Basic Pullover Sleeves (page 57), starting with a 1st rib row as for the Back, working in rib pattern throughout.

FINISHING

Join the shoulder seams. Sew on the sleeves, placing the center of the sleeves against the shoulder seams. Join the side and sleeve seams.

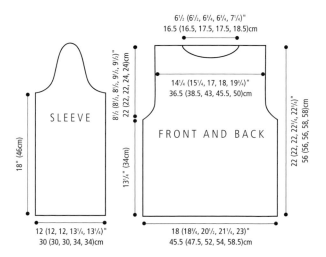

SLEEVE

8½ (8½, 8½, 9½, 9½)"
22 (22, 22, 24, 24)cm

18" (46cm)

13¼" (34cm)

12 (12, 12, 13¼, 13¼)"
30 (30, 30, 34, 34)cm

6½ (6½, 6¾, 6¾, 7¼)"
16.5 (16.5, 17.5, 17.5, 18.5)cm

14¼ (15¼, 17, 18, 19¾)"
36.5 (38.5, 43, 45.5, 50)cm

FRONT AND BACK

22 (22, 22, 22¾, 22¾)"
56 (56, 56, 58, 58)cm

18 (18¾, 20½, 21¼, 23)"
45.5 (47.5, 52, 54, 58.5)cm

CLASSIC JACKETS

basic jacket

1

The touch of silk and angora against the skin is pure luxury. The Basic Jacket, in sumptuous Kochoran, is knit in stockinette stitch and finished with a rib trimming along the edges. If you prefer your edges to lie flat not rolled, knit the last four stitches in garter stitch.

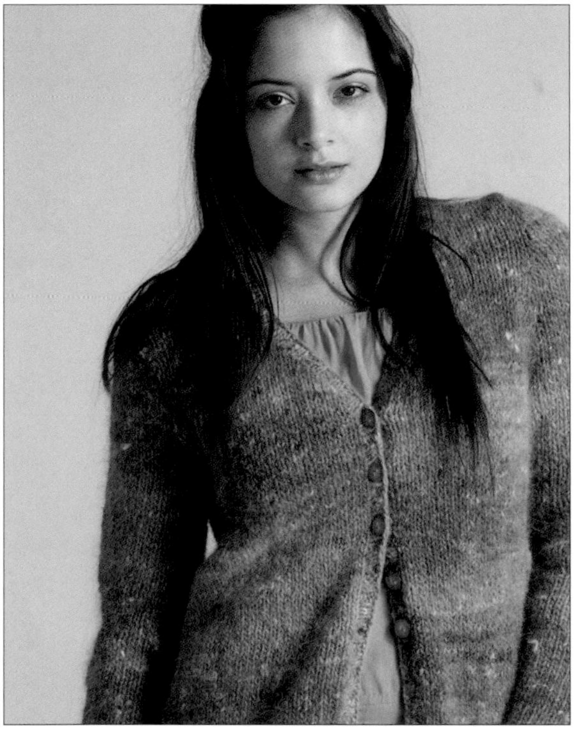

YARN TYPES

YARN

6 (7, 7, 7, 8) skeins of Noro Kochoran, 50% wool/20% silk/30% angora, 3½ oz (100g), each approximately 174 yds (160m), shade 10 (4) medium

5 buttons size ½" (1.5cm)

NEEDLES

One pair size 10 (6mm) knitting needles or size needed to obtain gauge

30" (80cm) long size 8 (5mm) circular knitting needle

GAUGE

16 stitches and 21 rows to 4" (10cm) square over stockinette stitch using size 10 (6mm) needles.

MEASUREMENTS

to fit chest

30–32	32–34	34–36	36–38	38–40 inches
76–81	81–86	86–91.5	91.5–96.5	96.5–101.5cm

actual measurement

34½	36½	38½	40¼	42¼ inches
87.5	92.5	97.5	102.5	107.5cm

length

28¼	28¼	28¼	29	29 inches
72	72	72	74	74cm

sleeve length

18	18	18	18	18 inches
46	46	46	46	46cm

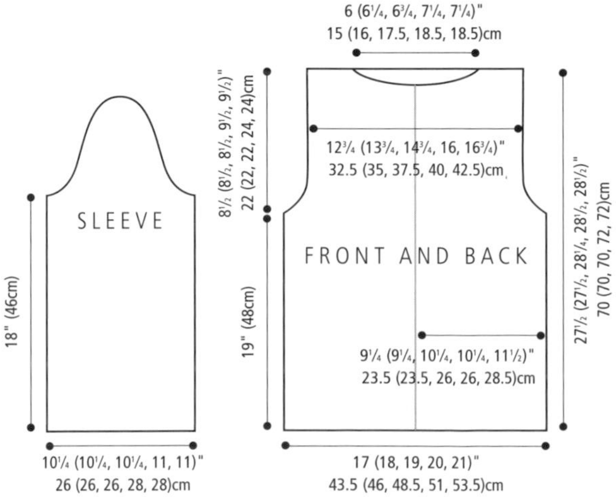
SLEEVE
18" (46cm)
10¼ (10¼, 10¼, 11, 11)"
26 (26, 26, 28, 28)cm
6 (6¼, 6¾, 7¼, 7¼)"
15 (16, 17.5, 18.5, 18.5)cm
8½ (8½, 8½, 9½, 9½)"
22 (22, 22, 24, 24)cm
12¾ (13¾, 14¾, 16, 16¾)"
32.5 (35, 37.5, 40, 42.5)cm
FRONT AND BACK
19" (48cm)
27½ (27½, 28¼, 28¼, 28½)"
70 (70, 70, 72, 72)cm
9¼ (9¼, 10¼, 10¼, 11½)"
23.5 (23.5, 26, 26, 28.5)cm
17 (18, 19, 20, 21)"
43.5 (46, 48.5, 51, 53.5)cm

BACK

With size 10 (6mm) needles, cast on 70 (74, 78, 82, 86) stitches.

Starting with a knit row, continue in stockinette stitch until the back measures 19¾" (50cm) from the cast-on edge, ending with a wrong-side row.

SHAPE ARMHOLES

Bind off 5 stitches at the beginning of the next 2 rows—60 (64, 68, 72, 76) stitches.

Decrease one stitch at each end of the next row. Then decrease one stitch at each end of every 4th row three times—52 (56, 60, 64, 68) stitches.

Continue without shaping in stockinette stitch until the armhole measures 7¾ (7¾, 7¾, 8½, 8½)" (20 [20, 20, 22, 22]cm) from the start of armhole shaping, ending with a wrong-side row.

SHAPE SHOULDERS

Bind off 14 (15, 16, 17, 19) stitches at the beginning of the next 2 rows.

Leave the center 24 (26, 28, 30, 30) stitches on a holder.

LEFT FRONT

With size 10 (6mm) needles, cast on 35 (37, 39, 41, 43) stitches.

Starting with a knit row, continue in stockinette stitch until the left front measures 19 ¾" (50cm) from the cast-on edge, ending with a wrong-side row.

SHAPE ARMHOLE AND NECK

Bind off 5 stitches at the beginning of the next row—30 (32, 34, 36, 38) stitches.

Work 1 row.

Decrease 1 stitch at the armhole edge of the next row. Then decrease 1 stitch at the armhole edge of every 4th row three times; **at the same time** decrease 1 stitch at the neck edge of the next and every other row until there are 14 (15, 16, 17, 19) stitches.

Continue without shaping in stockinette stitch until the armhole measures 8½ (8½, 8½, 9½, 9½)" (22 [22, 22, 24, 24]cm) from the start of the armhole shaping, ending with a wrong-side row. Bind off.

RIGHT FRONT

With size 10 (6mm) needles, cast on 35 (37, 39, 41, 43) stitches.

Starting with a knit row, continue in stockinette stitch until the work measures 19¾" (50cm) from the cast-on edge, ending with a right-side row.

SHAPE ARMHOLE AND NECK

Work as for Left Front Shape Armhole and Neck.

SLEEVES (MAKE TWO)

With size 10 (6mm) needles, cast on 42 (42, 42, 46, 46) stitches. Starting with a knit row, continue in stockinette stitch until the sleeve measures 18" (46cm) from the cast-on edge, ending with a wrong-side row.

SHAPE SLEEVE CAP

Bind off 5 stitches at the beginning of the next 2 rows—32 (32, 32, 36, 36) stitches.

Decrease 1 stitch at each end of the next row. Then decrease 1 stitch at each end of every 4th row four times—22 (22, 22, 26, 26) stitches.

Purl 1 row.

Decrease 1 stitch at each end of the next row. Then decrease 1 stitch at each end of every other row 3 times—14 (14, 14, 18, 18) stitches.

Work 3 (3, 3, 5, 5) rows in stockinette stitch.

Decrease 1 stitch at each end of the next and every following row until 8 (8, 8, 12, 12) stitches remain.

Bind off 3 stitches at the beginning of the next 2 rows—2 (2, 2, 6, 6) stitches.

Bind off the remaining stitches.

EDGING

Join the shoulder seams. With right side facing and size 8 (5mm) needles, pick up and k133 (134, 133, 136, 136) stitches up the right front and right front neck, k24 (26, 28, 30, 30) stitches from the holder at the center back, pick up and k133 (134, 133, 136, 136) stitches down the left front neck and left front—290 (294, 294, 302, 302) stitches.

Rib row P2, [k2, p2] to end.

Buttonhole row (right side) Work in rib for 20 stitches, *k2tog, yo, work in rib 6 stitches; repeat from * four times, k2tog, yo, work in rib to end.

Work in rib for 1 row.

Bind off.

FINISHING

Sew on the sleeves, placing the center of the sleeves against the shoulder seams. Join the side and sleeve seams. Position and sew buttons into place.

YARN TYPES ☐

YARN
4 (5, 5, 6, 6) skeins of Noro Kochoran, 50% wool/20% silk/30%angora, 3½ oz (100g), each approximately 174 yds (160m), shade 44 ④ medium

3 buttons size 1½" (3cm)

NEEDLES
One pair size 10 (6mm) knitting needles or size needed to obtain gauge
30" (80cm) long size 8 (5mm) circular knitting needle

GAUGE
16 stitches and 21 rows to 4" (10cm) square over stockinette stitch using size 10 (6mm) needles.

MEASUREMENTS

to fit chest

30–32	32–34	34–36	36–38	38–40 inches
76–81	81–86	86–91.5	91.5–96.5	96.5–101.5cm

actual measurement

34½	36½	38½	40¼	42¼ inches
87.5	92.5	97.5	102.5	107.5cm

length

22½	22½	22½	23¼	23¼ inches
57	57	57	59	59cm

sleeve length

10½	10½	10½	10½	10½ inches
27	27	27	27	27cm

cropped coat

When the mercury rises but evenings remain cool, look no further than this spring cover-up. This waist-length version of the basic cardigan features rib accents along waist and sleeves. I love this colorway, but I encourage you to work your favorite colors into the design for different results.

2

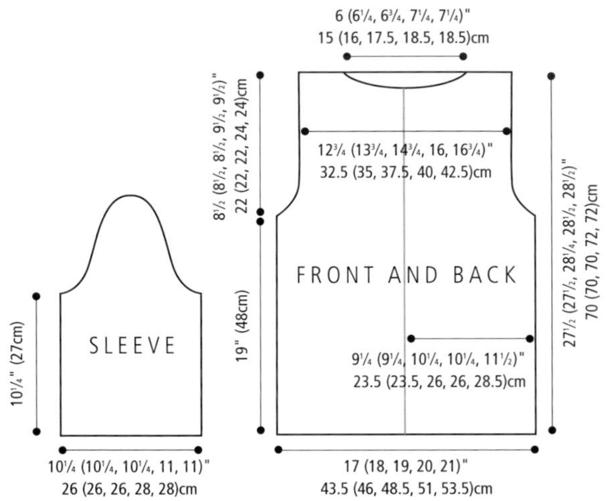
6 (6¼, 6¾, 7¼, 7¼)"
15 (16, 17.5, 18.5, 18.5)cm
8½ (8½, 8½, 9½, 9½)"
22 (22, 22, 24, 24)cm
12¾ (13¾, 14¾, 16, 16¾)"
32.5 (35, 37.5, 40, 42.5)cm
FRONT AND BACK
27½ (27½, 28¼, 28½, 28½)"
70 (70, 70, 72, 72)cm
SLEEVE
10¼" (27cm)
19" (48cm)
9¼ (9¼, 10¼, 10¼, 11½)"
23.5 (23.5, 26, 26, 28.5)cm
10¼ (10¼, 10¼, 11, 11)"
26 (26, 26, 28, 28)cm
17 (18, 19, 20, 21)"
43.5 (46, 48.5, 51, 53.5)cm

BACK

With size 10 (6mm) needles, cast on 70 (74, 78, 82, 86) stitches.
1st rib row (right side) K2, [p2, k2] to end.
2nd rib row P2, [k2, p2] to end.
These 2 rows form the rib pattern.
Repeat the last 2 rows until the back measures 8" (22cm) from the cast-on edge, ending with a wrong-side row.
Starting with a knit row, continue in stockinette stitch until the back measures 13¾" (35cm) from the cast-on edge, ending with a wrong-side row.

SHAPE ARMHOLES

Bind off 5 stitches at the beginning of the next 2 rows—60 (64, 68, 72, 76) stitches.
Decrease 1 stitch at each end of the next row. Then decrease 1 stitch at each end of every 4th row 3 times—52 (56, 60, 64, 68) stitches.
Continue without shaping in stockinette stitch until the armhole measures 8½ (8½, 8½, 9½, 9½)" (22 [22, 22, 24, 24]cm) from the start of the armhole shaping, ending with a wrong-side row.

SHAPE SHOULDERS

Bind off 14 (15, 16, 17, 19) stitches at the beginning of the next 2 rows.
Leave the center 24 (26, 28, 30, 30) stitches on a holder.

LEFT FRONT

With size 10 (6mm) needles, cast on 38 (38, 42, 42, 46) stitches.
1st rib row (right side) [K2, p2] to last 6 stitches, k6.
2nd rib row P6, [k2, p2] to end.
These 2 rows form the rib pattern with stockinette stitch edging.
Repeat the last 2 rows until the left front measures 8½" (22cm) from the cast-on edge, ending with a wrong-side row.
Starting with a knit row, continue in stockinette stitch until the left front measures 13¾" (35cm) from the cast-on edge, ending with a wrong-side row.

SHAPE ARMHOLE AND NECK

Bind off 5 stitches at the beginning of the next row. 33 (33, 37, 37, 41) stitches.
Purl 1 row.
Decrease 1 stitch at the armhole edge of the next row. Then decrease 1 stitch at the armhole edge of every 4th row 3 times; **at the same time** decrease 1 stitch at the neck edge of the next and every other row until there are 14 (15, 16, 17, 19) stitches.
Continue without shaping in stockinette stitch until the armhole measures 8½ (8½, 8½, 9½, 9½)" (22 [22, 22, 24, 24]cm) from the start of the armhole shaping, ending with a wrong-side row.
Bind off.

Mark the positions for 3 buttons along the front opening edge, positioning the first one 1" (3cm) from the cast-on edge and the last one 1" (3cm) before the start of the neck shaping and centering the remaining button in between.

RIGHT FRONT

With size 10 (6mm) needles, cast on 38 (38, 42, 42, 46) stitches.

1st rib row (right side) [K2, p2] to last 6 stitches, k6.

2nd rib row P6, [k2, p2] to end.

These 2 rows form the rib pattern with stockinette stitch edging. Repeat the last 2 rows until the right front measures 1" (3cm) from the cast-on edge, ending with a wrong-side row.

1st buttonhole row (right side) K2, bind off 2 stitches, work in pattern to end.

2nd buttonhole row Work in pattern to last 2 stitches, cast on 2 stitches, p2.

Continue in rib pattern with stockinette stitch edging and working buttonhole rows to correspond with button positions marked on the Left Front, until the right front measures 8½" (22cm) from the cast-on edge, ending with a wrong-side row. Starting with a knit row, continue in stockinette stitch and working remaining buttonhole row, until the right front measures 13¾" (35cm) from the cast-on edge, ending with a right-side row.

Work as for the Left Front Shape Armhole and Neck.

SLEEVES (MAKE TWO)

With size 10 (6mm) needles, cast on 42 (42, 42, 46, 46) stitches. Starting with a **1st rib row** as given for the Back, continue in rib pattern until the sleeve measures 4¾" (12cm) from the cast-on edge, ending with a wrong-side row.

Starting with a knit row, continue in stockinette stitch until the sleeve measures 10½" (27cm) from the cast-on edge, ending with a wrong-side row.

SHAPE SLEEVE CAP

Complete as for Basic Jacket Sleeves from Shape Sleeve Cap (page 77).

EDGING

Join the shoulder seams. With right side facing and a long size 8 (5mm) circular needle, pick up and k70 stitches up the right front, pick up and k39 (39, 39, 42, 42) stitches up the right front neck, k24 (26, 28, 30, 30) stitches from the holder at the center back, pick up and k 39 (39, 39, 42, 42) stitches down the left front neck, pick up and k70 stitches down the left front—242 (244, 246, 254, 254) stitches.
Bind off.

FINISHING

Sew on the sleeves, placing the center of the sleeves against the shoulder seams. Join the side and sleeve seams. Position and sew the buttons in place.

hooded jacket

Luxurious yet sporty, it's all about playing off the extremes. This hooded jacket is knit in garter stitch and has a close fit. Extend the length and add ribbing along the sleeves for an equally desirable look.

YARN TYPES

YARN
6 (7, 7, 8, 8) balls of Noro Kochoran, 50% wool/20% silk/30% angora, 3½ oz (100g), each approximately 174 yds (160m), in shade 50 (4) medium

Open-ended zipper to fit:
First 4 sizes: length 22" (57cm)
Last size: length 23" (59cm)

NEEDLES
One pair size 10 (6mm) knitting needles or size needed to obtain gauge

GAUGE
16 stitches and 21 rows to 4" (10cm) square over stockinette stitch using size 10 (6mm) needles.

MEASUREMENTS

to fit chest

30–32	32–34	34–36	36–38	38–40 inches
76–81	81–86	86–91.5	91.5–96.5	96.5–101.5cm

actual measurement

34½	36½	38½	40¼	42¼ inches
87.5	92.5	97.5	102.5	107.5cm

length

22½	22½	22½	23¼	23¼ inches
57	57	57	59	59cm

sleeve length

18	18	18	18	18 inches
46	46	46	46	46cm

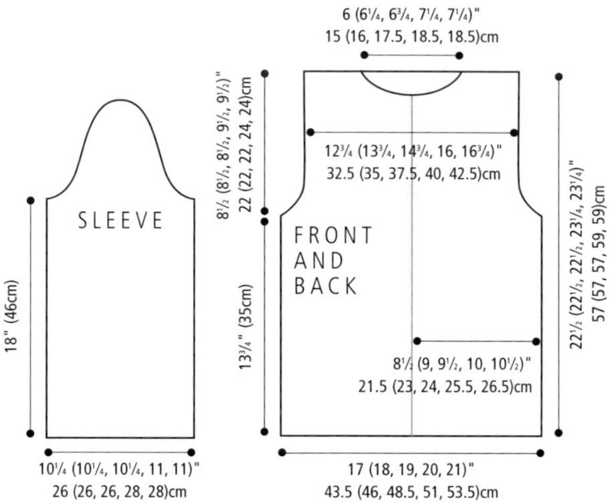
6 (6¼, 6¾, 7¼, 7¼)"
15 (16, 17.5, 18.5, 18.5)cm
SLEEVE
18" (46cm)
10¼ (10¼, 10¼, 11, 11)"
26 (26, 26, 28, 28)cm
8½ (8½, 8½, 9½, 9½)"
22 (22, 22, 24, 24)cm
12¾ (13¾, 14¾, 16, 16¾)"
32.5 (35, 37.5, 40, 42.5)cm
FRONT AND BACK
13¾" (35cm)
8½ (9, 9½, 10, 10½)"
21.5 (23, 24, 25.5, 26.5)cm
22½ (22½, 22½, 23¼, 23¼)"
57 (57, 57, 59, 59)cm
17 (18, 19, 20, 21)"
43.5 (46, 48.5, 51, 53.5)cm

BACK

With size 10 (6mm) needles, cast on 70 (74, 78, 82, 86) stitches.

Starting with a knit row, work 6 rows in stockinette stitch.

Starting with a knit row, continue in garter stitch until the back measures 13¾" (35cm) from the cast-on edge, ending with a wrong-side row.

SHAPE ARMHOLES

Bind off 5 stitches at the beginning of the next 2 rows—60 (64, 68, 72, 76) stitches.

Decrease 1 stitch at the armhole edge of the next row. Then decrease 1 stitch at the armhole edge of every 4th row 3 times—52 (56, 60, 64, 68) stitches.

Continue without shaping in garter stitch until the armhole measures 8½ (8½, 8½, 9½, 9½)" (22 [22, 22, 24, 24]cm) from the start of the armhole shaping, ending with a wrong-side row.

SHAPE SHOULDERS

Bind off 14 (15, 16, 17, 19) stitches at the beginning of the next 2 rows.

Leave the center 24 (26, 28, 30, 30) stitches on a holder.

LEFT FRONT

With size 10 (6mm) needles, cast on 35 (37, 39, 41, 43) stitches.

Starting with a knit row, work 6 rows in stockinette stitch.

Starting with a knit row, continue in garter stitch until the left front measures 13¾" (35cm) from the cast-on edge, ending with a wrong-side row.

SHAPE ARMHOLE

Bind off 5 stitches at the beginning of the next row. 30 (32, 34, 36, 38) stitches.

Knit 1 row.

Decrease 1 stitch at the armhole edge of the next row. Then decrease 1 stitch at the armhole edge of every 4th row 3 times—26 (28, 30, 32, 34) stitches.

Continue without shaping in garter stitch until the armhole measures 7 (7, 7, 8, 8)" (18 [18, 18, 20, 20]cm) from the start of the armhole shaping, ending with a right-side row.

SHAPE NECK

K8 (9, 10, 11, 11) stitches, slip these stitches onto a holder, knit to end—18 (19, 20, 21, 23) stitches.

Decrease 1 stitch at the neck edge of the next and every following row until there are 14 (15, 16, 17, 19) stitches.

Continue without shaping in garter stitch until the armhole measures 8½ (8½, 8½, 9½, 9½)" (22 [22, 22, 24, 24]cm) from the start of the armhole shaping, ending with a wrong-side row.

Bind off.

RIGHT FRONT

With size 10 (6mm) needles, cast on 35 (37, 39, 41, 43) stitches.

Starting with a knit row, work 6 rows in stockinette stitch.

Starting with a knit row, continue in garter stitch until the right front measures 13¾" (35cm) from the cast-on edge, ending with a right-side row.

SHAPE ARMHOLE

Bind off 5 stitches at the beginning of the next row. 30 (32, 34, 36, 38) stitches.

Knit 1 row.

Decrease 1 stitch at the armhole edge of the next and 3 following 4th rows. 26 (28, 30, 32, 34) stitches.

Continue without shaping in garter stitch until the armhole measures 7 (7, 7, 8, 8)" (18 [18, 18, 20, 20]cm) from the start of the armhole shaping, ending with a wrong-side row.

Work as for Left Front Shape Neck.

SLEEVES (MAKE TWO)

Work as for Basic Jacket Sleeves (page 77), working the first 6 rows in stockinette stitch and then completing the sleeves in garter stitch throughout.

HOOD

Join the shoulder seams. With right side facing and size 10 (6mm) needles, k8 (9, 10, 11, 11) stitches from the holder at the right front, pick up and k8 stitches up the right front neck, k24 (26, 28, 30, 30) stitches from the holder at the center back, pick up and knit 8 stitches along the left front neck, k8 (9, 10, 11, 11) stitches from the holder at the left front—56 (60, 64, 68, 68) stitches.

Starting with a knit row, continue in garter stitch until the hood measures 5½" (14cm), ending with a wrong-side row.

Next row K16 (17, 18, 19, 19), m1, k1, m1, knit to last 17 (18, 19, 20, 20) stitches, m1, k1, m1, knit to end.

Knit 3 rows.

Next row K17 (18, 19, 20, 20) stitches, m1, k1, m1, knit to last 18 (19, 20, 21, 21) stitches, m1, k1, m1, knit to end.

Continue without shaping in garter stitch until the hood measures 13¾" (35cm), ending with a wrong-side row.

Bind off.

FINISHING

With right sides together, join the bound-off edges of the hood. Sew on the sleeves, placing the center of the sleeves against the shoulder seams. Join the side and sleeve seams. Position and sew the zipper in place.

cowl cover-up

With a wide boat neck and cowl-inspired front, this garter-stitched cardigan is unique, comfortable, and thoroughly modern. The unusual coloring effects are produced by knitting with two strands of yarn held together, and though it has no zipper or buttons, a decorative antique brooch or oversized safety pin would make ideal closures.

YARN TYPES

YARN
6 (7, 7, 8, 8) balls of Noro Kochoran, 50% wool/20% silk/30% angora, 3½ oz (100g), each approximately 174 yds (160m), shade 54 (4) medium

NEEDLES
One pair size 10 (6mm) knitting needles or size needed to obtain gauge

GAUGE
16 stitches and 26 rows to 4" (10cm) square over garter stitch using size 10 (6mm) needles.

MEASUREMENTS

to fit chest

30–32	32–34	34–36	36–38	38–40 inches
76–81	81–86	86–91.5	91.5–96.5	96.5–101.5cm

actual measurement

34½	36½	38½	40¼	42¼ inches
87.5	92.5	97.5	102.5	107.5cm

length

22½	22½	22½	23¼	23¼ inches
57	57	57	59	59cm

sleeve length

10½	10½	10½	10½	10½ inches
27	27	27	27	27cm

4

NOTE

It is very important to get the correct row gauge for this garment, as the increase rows at the front edge finish before you bind off for the neck.

BACK

With size 10 (6mm) needles, cast on 70 (74, 78, 82, 86) stitches.

Starting with a knit row, continue in garter stitch until the back measures 13¾" (35cm) from the cast-on edge, ending with a wrong-side row.

SHAPE ARMHOLES

Complete as for Hooded Jacket Back from Shape Armholes (page 84).

LEFT FRONT

With size 10 (6mm) needles, cast on 25 (26, 27, 28, 29) stitches.

Knit 2 rows.

Increase row Knit to last 3 stitches, m1, k2.

Continue in garter stitch, increasing 1 stitch at the front edge every 3rd row until the left front measures 13¾" (35cm), ending with a wrong-side row.

Continue to increase 1 stitch at the front edge every 3rd row; **and at the same time** shape the armhole as follows:

SHAPE ARMHOLE

Bind off 5 stitches at the beginning of the next row.

Knit 1 row.

Decrease 1 stitch at the armhole edge of the next row. Then decrease 1 stitch at the armhole edge of every 4th row 3 times.

Continue to increase 1 stitch at the front edge every 3rd row until there are 54 (56, 58, 60, 62) stitches.

Continue without shaping in garter stitch until the armhole measures 8½ (8½, 8½, 9½, 9½)" (22 [22, 22, 24, 24]cm) from the start of the armhole shaping, ending with a right-side row.

Next row Bind off 40 (41, 42, 43, 43) stitches, knit to end.

Bind off.

RIGHT FRONT

With size 10 (6mm) needles, cast on 25 (26, 27, 28, 29) stitches.

Knit 2 rows.

Increase row K2, m1, knit to end.

Continue in garter stitch, increasing 1 stitch at the front edge every 3rd row, until the right front measures 13¾" (35cm), ending with a right-side row.

Continue to increase 1 stitch at the front edge every 3rd row; and **at the same time** work as for the Left Front Shape Armhole.

SLEEVES (MAKE TWO)

With size 10 (6mm) needles, cast on 42 (42, 42, 46, 46) stitches.

Work in garter stitch until the sleeve measures 10½" (27cm) from the cast-on edge, ending with a wrong-side row.

SHAPE SLEEVE CAP

Complete as for Basic Jacket Sleeves from Shape Sleeve Cap (page 77).

FINISHING

Join the shoulder seams. Sew on the sleeves, placing the center of the sleeves against the shoulder seams. Join the side and sleeve seams.

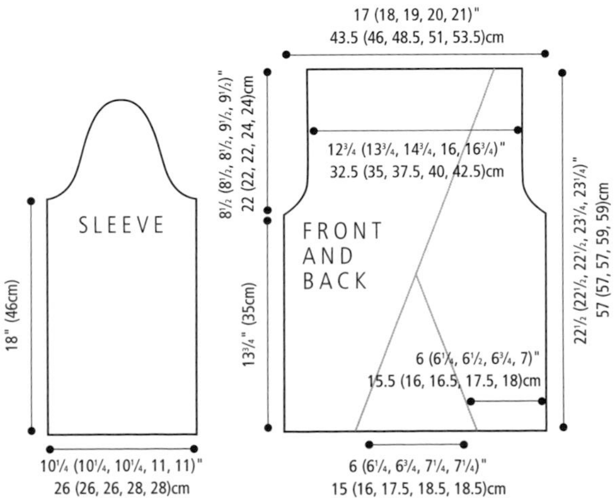
17 (18, 19, 20, 21)"
43.5 (46, 48.5, 51, 53.5)cm
SLEEVE
18" (46cm)
10¼ (10¼, 10¼, 11, 11)"
26 (26, 26, 28, 28)cm
8½ (8½, 8½, 9½, 9½)"
22 (22, 22, 24, 24)cm
13¾" (35cm)
12¾ (13¾, 14¾, 16, 16¾)"
32.5 (35, 37.5, 40, 42.5)cm
FRONT
AND
BACK
6 (6¼, 6½, 6¾, 7)"
15.5 (16, 16.5, 17.5, 18)cm
6 (6¼, 6¾, 7¼, 7¼)"
15 (16, 17.5, 18.5, 18.5)cm
22½ (22½, 22½, 23¼, 23¼)"
57 (57, 57, 59, 59)cm

long coat

There's no reason to be left out in the cold with this striking winter wrap. It has a wonderful allover rib pattern, and the 3-button closure offers a design detail that sets it apart from the rest. This fetching coat will keep you looking your best day to night.

YARN TYPES

YARN
4 (4, 4, 10, 10) balls of Noro Kochoran, 50% wool/20% silk/30% angora, 3½ oz (100g), each approximately 174 yds (160m), shade 10 (A) [4] medium

4 (4, 4, 10, 10) balls of Noro Kochoran, 50% wool/20% silk/30% angora, 3½ oz (100g), each approximately 174 yds (160m), shade 50 (B) [4] medium

3 buttons size 1½" (3cm)

NEEDLES
One pair size 10 (6mm) knitting needles or size needed to obtain gauge

GAUGE
16 stitches and 21 rows to 4" (10cm) square over stockinette stitch using size 10 (6mm) needles.

MEASUREMENTS
to fit chest

30–32	32–34	34–36	36–38	38–40 inches
76–81	81–86	86–91.5	91.5–96.5	96.5–101.5cm

actual measurement

34½	36½	38½	40¼	42¼ inches
87.5	92.5	97.5	102.5	107.5cm

length

30¾	30¾	30¾	31½	31½ inches
78	78	78	80	80cm

sleeve length

18	18	18	18	18 inches
46	46	46	46	46cm

5

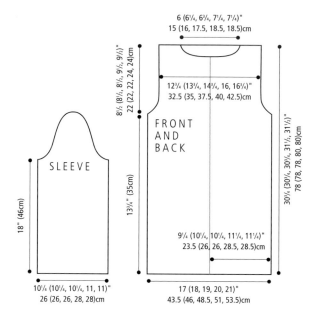

SLEEVE

18" (46cm)

10¼ (10¼, 10¼, 11, 11)"
26 (26, 26, 28, 28)cm

6 (6¼, 6¾, 7¼, 7¼)"
15 (16, 17.5, 18.5, 18.5)cm

8½ (8½, 8½, 9½, 9½)"
22 (22, 22, 24, 24)cm

12¾ (13¾, 14¾, 16, 16¾)"
32.5 (35, 37.5, 40, 42.5)cm

FRONT AND BACK

13¾" (35cm)

30¾ (30¾, 30¾, 31½, 31½)"
78 (78, 78, 80, 80)cm

9¼ (10¼, 10¼, 11¼, 11¼)"
23.5 (26, 26, 28.5, 28.5)cm

17 (18, 19, 20, 21)"
43.5 (46, 48.5, 51, 53.5)cm

2-ROW STRIPED PATTERN

Work 2 rows in B.

Work 2 rows in A.

These 2 rows form the striped pattern; repeat throughout.

BACK

With size 10 (6mm) needles and yarn A, cast on 70 (74, 78, 82, 86) stitches.

Knit 3 rows.

1st pattern row (right side) Knit.

2nd pattern row P2, [k2, p2] to end.

These 2 rows form the garter stitch rib pattern.

Repeat the last 2 rows and striped pattern until the back measures 22" (56cm) from the cast-on edge, ending with a wrong-side row.

SHAPE ARMHOLES

Bind off 5 stitches at the beginning of the next 2 rows—60 (64, 68, 72, 76) stitches.

Decrease 1 stitch at the armhole edge of the next row. Then decrease 1 stitch at the armhole edge of every 4th row 3 times—52 (56, 60, 64, 68) stitches.

Continue without shaping in garter stitch rib and striped pattern until the armhole measures 8½ (8½, 8½, 9½, 9½)" (22 [22, 22, 24, 24]cm) from the start of the armhole shaping, ending with a wrong-side row.

SHAPE SHOULDERS

Bind off 14 (15, 16, 17, 19) stitches at the beginning of the next 2 rows.

Leave the center 24 (26, 28, 30, 30) stitches on a holder.

LEFT FRONT

With size 10 (6mm) needles and yarn A, cast on 38 (42, 42, 46, 46) stitches.

Knit 3 rows.

1st pattern row (right side) Knit.

2nd pattern row K4, p2, [k2, p2] to end.

These 2 rows form the garter stitch rib pattern.

Repeat the last 2 rows and striped pattern until the left front measures 22" (56cm) from the cast-on edge, ending with a wrong-side row.

SHAPE ARMHOLE

Bind off 5 stitches at the beginning of the next row—33 (37, 37, 41, 41) stitches.

Work 1 row in striped pattern.

Decrease 1 stitch at the armhole edge of the next row. Then decrease 1 stitch at the armhole edge of every 4th row 3 times—29 (33, 33, 37, 37) stitches.

Continue without shaping in garter stitch rib and striped pattern until the armhole measures 7 (7, 7, 7¾, 7¾)" (18 [18, 18, 20, 20]cm) from the start of the armhole shaping, ending with a right-side row.

SHAPE NECK

Work 11 (14, 13, 16, 14) stitches, slip these stitches onto a holder, work to end.

Decrease 1 stitch at the neck edge of the next and every following row until there are 14 (15, 16, 17, 19) stitches.

Continue without shaping in garter stitch rib and striped pattern until the armhole measures 8½ (8½, 8½, 9½, 9½)" (22 [22, 22, 24, 24]cm) from the start of the armhole shaping, ending with a wrong-side row.

Bind off.

RIGHT FRONT

With size 10 (6mm) needles and yarn A, cast on 38 (42, 42, 46, 46) stitches.

Knit 3 rows.

1st pattern row (right side) Knit.

2nd pattern row K4, p2, [k2, p2] to end.

These 2 rows form the garter stitch rib pattern.

Repeat the last 2 rows and striped pattern until the right front measures 22" (56cm) from the cast-on edge, ending with a right-side row.

Work as for Left Front Shape Armhole.

SLEEVES (MAKE TWO)

Work as for Basic Jacket Sleeves (page 77), working the first 4 rows in garter stitch and then, starting with a 1st pattern row as given for the Back, completing the sleeves in garter stitch rib throughout.

COLLAR

Join the shoulder seams. With right side facing, size 10 (6mm) needles and A, k11 (14, 13, 16, 14) stitches from the holder at the right front, pick up and k8 (8, 8, 10, 10) stitches up the right front neck, k24 (26, 28, 30, 30) stitches from the holder at the center back, pick up and k8 (8, 8, 10, 10) stitches along the left front neck, k11 (14, 13, 16, 14) stitches from the holder at the left front—62 (70, 70, 82, 78) stitches.

1st pattern row K4, p2, [k2, p2] to last 4 stitches, k4.

2nd pattern row Knit.

These 2 rows form the garter stitch rib pattern.

Work 1st pattern row once.

1st buttonhole row (right side) K1, bind off 2 stitches, knit to end.

2nd buttonhole row Work in pattern to last stitch, cast on 2 stitches, k1.

Work 6 rows in pattern.

Repeat the last 8 rows once more, then work the 1st and 2nd buttonhole rows once more.

Continue to work in pattern until collar measures 4¾" (12cm), ending with a wrong-side row.

Bind off.

FINISHING

Sew on the sleeves, placing the center of the sleeves against the shoulder seams. Join the side and sleeve seams. Position and sew the buttons in place.

FITTED CARDIGANS

basic fitted cardigan

Simple yet stylish, fitted yet comfortable, this figure-flattering cardigan is another great wardrobe addition. The style is worked in an eye-popping explosion of rainbow hues and can be redesigned to create a bespoke garment to call your own. Ribbed sleeves? New stitch pattern? Different neckline? The possibilities are only limited to your imagination.

1

YARN

8 (8, 9, 9, 10) balls of Noro Silk Garden, 45% silk/45% mohair/10% lambswool, 1¾ oz (50g), each approximately 110 yds (100m), shade 205 (4) medium

10 buttons size ¼" (6mm)

NEEDLES

One pair size 8 (5mm) knitting needles or size needed to obtain gauge
One pair size 6 (4mm) knitting needles

GAUGE

18 stitches and 24 rows to 4" (10cm) square over stockinette stitch using size 8 (5mm) needles.

MEASUREMENTS
to fit chest

32–34	34–36	36–38	40–42	42–44 inches
81–86	86–91.5	91.5–96.5	101.5–106.5	106.5–111.5cm

actual measurement

35¾	37½	41	43	46¼ inches
91	95.5	104.5	109	117.5cm

length

22	22	22	22¾	22¾ inches
56	56	56	58	58cm

sleeve length

18	18	18	18	18 inches
46	46	46	46	46cm

BACK

With size 8 (5mm) needles, cast on 82 (86, 94, 98 106) stitches. Starting with a knit row, continue in stockinette stitch until the back measures 13½" (34.5cm) from the cast-on edge, ending with a wrong-side row.

SHAPE ARMHOLES

Bind off 4 stitches at the beginning of the next 2 rows—74 (78, 86, 90, 98) stitches.
Decrease 1 stitch at each end of the next row. Then decrease 1 stitch at each end of every 4th row 3 times—66 (70, 78, 82, 90) stitches.
Continue in stockinette stitch without shaping until the armhole measures 8½ (8½, 8½, 9½, 9½)" (22 [22, 22, 24, 24]cm) from the start of the armhole shaping, ending with a wrong side row.

SHAPE SHOULDERS

Bind off 18 (20, 23, 25, 28) stitches at the beginning of the next 2 rows.
Leave the remaining 30 (30, 32, 32, 34) stitches on a holder.

LEFT FRONT

With size 8 (5mm) needles, cast on 41 (43, 47, 49, 53) stitches. Starting with a knit row, continue in stockinette stitch without shaping until the left front measures 13½" (34.5cm) from the cast on edge, ending with a wrong-side row.

SHAPE ARMHOLE

Bind off 4 stitches at the beginning of the next row—37 (39, 43, 45, 49) stitches.
Purl 1 row.
Decrease 1 stitch at each end of the next row. Then decrease 1 stitch at each end of every 4th row 3 times—33 (35, 39, 41, 45) stitches.
Continue in stockinette stitch without shaping until the armhole measures 5½ (5½, 5½, 6¼, 6¼)" (14 [14, 14, 16, 16]cm) from the start of the armhole shaping, ending with a right-side row.

SHAPE NECK

Next row P11 (11, 12, 12, 13), slip these stitches onto a holder, purl to end—22 (24, 27, 29, 32) stitches.
Decrease 1 stitch at the neck edge of the next row and then every other row until 18 (20, 23, 25, 28) stitches remain.
Continue in stockinette stitch without shaping until the armhole measures 8½ (8½, 8½, 9½, 9½)" (22 [22, 22, 24, 24]cm) from the start of the armhole shaping, ending with a wrong-side row.
Bind off.

RIGHT FRONT

With size 8 (5mm) needles, cast on 41 (43, 47, 49, 53) stitches. Starting with a knit row, continue in stockinette stitch without shaping until the right front measures 13½" (34.5cm) from the cast-on edge, ending with a right-side row.

SHAPE ARMHOLE

Bind off 4 stitches at the beginning of the next row—37 (39, 43, 45, 49) stitches.
Knit 1 row.
Decrease 1 stitch at each end of the next row. Then decrease 1 stitch at each end of every 4th row 3 times—33 (35, 39, 41, 45) stitches.
Continue in stockinette stitch without shaping until the armhole measures 5½ (5½, 5½, 6¼, 6¼)" (14 [14, 14, 16, 16]cm) from the start of the armhole shaping, ending with a wrong-side row. Complete as for Left Front from Shape Neck.

SLEEVES (MAKE TWO)

With size 8 (5mm) needles, cast on 54 (54, 54, 62, 62) stitches. Starting with a knit row, continue in stockinette stitch until the sleeve measures 18" (46cm) from the cast-on edge, ending with a wrong-side row.

SHAPE SLEEVE CAP

Bind off 4 stitches at the beginning of the next 2 rows. 46 (46, 46, 54, 54) stitches.
Work 2 rows in stockinette stitch.
Decrease 1 stitch at each end of the next row. Then decrease 1 stitch at each end of every 4th row 5 times—34 (34, 34, 42, 42) stitches.
Purl 1 row.
Decrease 1 stitch at each end of the next row and then every other row twice—28 (28, 28, 36, 36) stitches.
Work 3 (3, 5, 5) rows in stockinette stitch.
Decrease 1 stitch at each end of the next and every following row until 18 (18, 18, 22, 22) stitches remain.
Bind off 4 stitches at the beginning of the next 2 rows. 10 (10, 10, 14, 14) stitches.
Bind off the remaining stitches.

NECK EDGING

Join shoulder seams. With right side facing and size 6 (4mm) needles, k11 (11, 12, 12, 13) stitches from the holder at the right front, pick up and k19 (19, 19, 21, 21) stitches up the right front neck, k30 (30, 32, 32, 34) stitches from the holder at the center back, pick up and k19 (19, 19, 21, 21) stitches down the left front neck, k11 (11, 12, 12, 13) stitches from the holder at the left front—90 (90, 94, 98, 102) stitches.
Knit 2 rows.
Bind off.

LEFT EDGING

With right side facing and size 6 (4mm) needles, pick up and knit 105 stitches down the left front opening edge.
Knit 1 row.
Bind off.

RIGHT EDGING

With right side facing and size 6 (4mm) needles, pick up and knit 105 stitches up the right front opening edge.
Knit 1 row.
Buttonhole row K2, *yo, k2tog, k9; repeat from * to last 4 stitches, yo, k2tog, k2.
Bind off loosely.

FINISHING

Sew on the sleeves, placing the center of the sleeves against the shoulder seams. Join the side and sleeve seams. Position and sew the buttons in place.

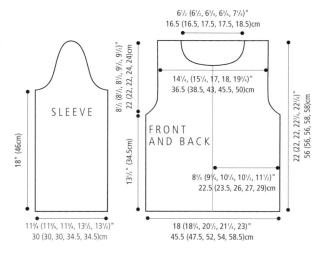

SLEEVE

18" (46cm)

8½ (8½, 8½, 9½, 9½)"
22 (22, 22, 24, 24)cm

11¾ (11¾, 11¾, 13½, 13½)"
30 (30, 30, 34.5, 34.5)cm

6½ (6½, 6¾, 6¾, 7¼)"
16.5 (16.5, 17.5, 17.5, 18.5)cm

14¼ (15¼, 17, 18, 19¾)"
36.5 (38.5, 43, 45.5, 50)cm

FRONT AND BACK

13½" (34.5cm)

22 (22, 22, 22¾, 22¾)"
56 (56, 56, 58, 58)cm

8¾ (9¼, 10¼, 10½, 11½)"
22.5 (23.5, 26, 27, 29)cm

18 (18¾, 20½, 21¼, 23)"
45.5 (47.5, 52, 54, 58.5)cm

rib detail cardigan

Remember, a gorgeous cardigan knit in a wooly yarn is the chic alternative to a coat. This unassuming design with ¾-length sleeves has been reincarnated with the addition of rib detailing along the waistline, cuffs, and edges.

YARN TYPES

YARN
9 (9, 10, 10, 11) balls of Noro Kureyon, 100% wool, 1¾ oz (50g), each approximately 110yd (100m), shade 188 [4] medium

10 buttons size ¼" (6mm)

NEEDLES
One pair size 8 (5mm) knitting needles or size needed to obtain gauge
One pair size 6 (4mm) knitting needles

GAUGE
18 stitches and 24 rows to 4" (10cm) square over stockinette stitch using size 8 (5mm) needles.

MEASUREMENTS
to fit chest

32–34	34–36	36–38	40–42	42–44 inches
81–86	86–91.5	91.5–96.5	101.5–106.5	106.5–111.5cm

actual measurement

35¾	37½	41	43	46¼ inches
91	95.5	104.5	109	117.5cm

length

22	22	22	22¾	22¾ inches
56	56	56	58	58cm

sleeve length

10½	10½	10½	10½	10½ inches
27	27	27	27	27cm

2

BACK

With size 8 (5mm) needles, cast on 82 (86, 94, 98, 106) stitches.

1st rib row K2, [p2, k2] to end.
2nd rib row P2, [k2, p2] to end.
These 2 rows form the rib pattern.
Repeat the last 2 rows until the back measures 9½" (24cm) from the cast-on edge, ending with a wrong-side row.
Starting with a knit row, continue in stockinette stitch until the back measures 13¼" (34cm) from the cast-on edge, ending with a wrong-side row.

SHAPE ARMHOLES

Work as for Basic Fitted Cardigan Back from Shape Armholes (page 97).

LEFT FRONT

With size 8 (5mm) needles, cast on 41 (43, 47, 49, 53) stitches.
1st rib row K0 (2, 2, 0, 0), [p2, k2] to last stitch, k1.
2nd rib row P3, k2, [p2, k2] to last 0 (2, 2, 0, 0) stitches, purl to end.
These 2 rows form the rib pattern.
Repeat the last 2 rows until the left front measures 9½" (24cm) from the cast-on edge, ending with a wrong-side row.
Starting with a knit row, continue in stockinette stitch until the left front measures 13¼" (34cm) from the cast-on edge, ending with a wrong-side row.

SHAPE ARMHOLE

Work as for Basic Fitted Cardigan Left Front from Shape Armholes (page 97).

RIGHT FRONT

With size 8 (5mm) needles, cast on 41 (43, 47, 49, 53) stitches.

1st rib row K1, [k2, p2] to last 0 (2, 2, 0, 0) stitches; knit to end.
2nd rib row P0 (2, 2, 0, 0), k2, [p2, k2] to last 3 stitches, p3.
These 2 rows form the rib pattern.
Repeat the last 2 rows until the right front measures 9½" (24cm) from the cast-on edge, ending with a wrong-side row.
Starting with a knit row, continue in stockinette stitch until the right front measures 13¼" (34cm) from the cast-on edge, ending with a right-side row.

SHAPE ARMHOLE

Work as for Basic Fitted Cardigan Right Front from Shape Armhole (page 99).

SLEEVES (MAKE TWO)

With size 8 (5mm) needles, cast on 54 (54, 54, 62, 62) stitches.
Starting with a 1st rib row, continue in rib pattern until the sleeve measures 2" (5cm) from the cast-on edge, ending with a wrong-side row.
Starting with a knit row, continue in stockinette stitch until the sleeve measures 10½" (27cm) from the cast-on edge, ending with a wrong-side row.

SHAPE SLEEVE CAP

Work as for Basic Fitted Cardigan Sleeves from Shape Sleeve Cap (page 99).

NECK EDGING

Join the shoulder seams. With right side facing and using size 6 (4mm) needles, k11 (11, 12, 12, 13) stitches from the holder at the right front, pick up and k19 (19, 19, 21, 21) stitches up the right front neck, k30 (30, 32, 32, 34) stitches from the holder at the center back, pick up and k19 (19, 19, 21, 21) stitches down the left front neck, k11 (11, 12, 12, 13) stitches from the holder at the left front—90 (90, 94, 98, 102) stitches.
Starting with a 2nd rib row as given for the Back, continue in rib pattern until the neck edging measures ¾" (2cm), ending with a wrong-side row.
Bind off.

LEFT EDGING

Work as for Basic Fitted Cardigan Left Edging (page 99).

RIGHT EDGING

Work as for Basic Fitted Cardigan Right Edging (page 99).

FINISHING

Sew on the sleeves, placing the center of the sleeves against the shoulder seams. Join the side and sleeve seams. Position and sew the buttons in place.

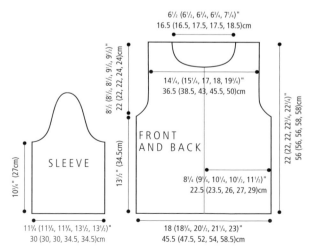

6½ (6½, 6¾, 6¾, 7¼)"
16.5 (16.5, 17.5, 17.5, 18.5)cm

8½ (8½, 8½, 9½, 9½)"
22 (22, 22, 24, 24)cm

14¼, (15¼, 17, 18, 19¼)"
36.5 (38.5, 43, 45.5, 50)cm

10¼" (27cm)

SLEEVE

13½" (34.5cm)

FRONT AND BACK

22 (22, 22, 22¼, 22¾)"
56 (56, 56, 58, 58)cm

8¾ (9¼, 10¼, 10½, 11½)"
22.5 (23.5, 26, 27, 29)cm

11¼ (11¾, 11¾, 13½, 13½)"
30 (30, 30, 34.5, 34.5)cm

18 (18¾, 20½, 21¼, 23)"
45.5 (47.5, 52, 54, 58.5)cm

cardigan with pockets

There is no other yarn that stripes quite like Noro—keep the knits simple and let the yarn do the work. In this cardigan, the stockinette-stitched fabric is balanced out with cool ribbing along the edges. The design is completed with two pockets accented with button closures.

3

YARN TYPES

YARN

9 (9, 10, 10, 11) balls of Noro Silk Garden, 45% silk/45% mohair/10% lambswool, 1¾ oz (50g) each approximately 110 yds (100m), shade 8 (4) medium

8 buttons size ½" (1.5cm)

NEEDLES

One pair size 8 (5mm) knitting needles or size needed to obtain gauge

One pair size 6 (4mm) knitting needles

GAUGE

18 stitches and 24 rows to 4" (10cm) square over stockinette stitch using size 8 (5mm) needles.

MEASUREMENTS

to fit chest

32–34	34–36	36–38	40–42	42–44 inches
81–86	86–91.5	91.5–96.5	101.5–106.5	106.5–111.5cm

actual measurement

35¾	37½	41	43	46¼ inches
91	95.5	104.5	109	117.5cm

length

22	22	22	22¾	22¾ inches
56	56	56	58	58cm

sleeve length

18	18	18	18	18 inches
46	46	46	46	46cm

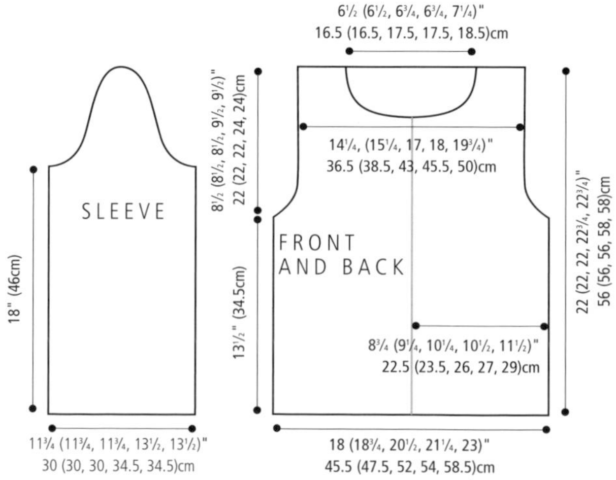
6½ (6½, 6¾, 6¾, 7¼)"
16.5 (16.5, 17.5, 17.5, 18.5)cm
8½ (8½, 8½, 9½, 9½)"
22 (22, 22, 24, 24)cm
14¼ (15¼, 17, 18, 19¾)"
36.5 (38.5, 43, 45.5, 50)cm
SLEEVE
FRONT AND BACK
18" (46cm)
13½" (34.5cm)
22 (22, 22, 22¾, 22¾)"
56 (56, 56, 58, 58)cm
8¾ (9¼, 10¼, 10½, 11½)"
22.5 (23.5, 26, 27, 29)cm
11¾ (11¾, 11¾, 13½, 13½)"
30 (30, 30, 34.5, 34.5)cm
18 (18¾, 20½, 21¼, 23)"
45.5 (47.5, 52, 54, 58.5)cm

BACK

With size 8 (5mm) needles, cast on 82 (86, 94, 98, 106) stitches.

1st rib row K2, [p2, k2] to end.

2nd rib row P2, [k2, p2] to end.

These 2 rows form the rib pattern.

Repeat the last 2 rows until the back measures 4" (10cm) from the cast-on edge, ending with a wrong-side row.

Starting with a knit row, continue in stockinette stitch until the back measures 13¼" (34cm) from the cast-on edge, ending with a wrong-side row.

SHAPE ARMHOLES

Work as for Basic Fitted Cardigan Back from Shape Armholes (page 97).

POCKET LININGS (MAKE TWO)

With size 8 (5mm) needles, cast on 18 stitches.

Starting with the 1st rib row as given for the Back, continue in rib pattern until the pocket lining measures 4¾" (12cm) from the cast-on edge, ending with a wrong-side row.

Place the stitches on a holder.

LEFT FRONT

With size 8 (5mm) needles, cast on 41 (43, 47, 49, 53) stitches.

1st rib row K0 (2, 2, 0, 0), [p2, k2] to last stitch, k1.

2nd rib row P3, k2, [p2, k2] to last 0 (2, 2, 0, 0) stitches, purl to end.

These 2 rows form the rib pattern.

Repeat the last 2 rows until the left front measures 4" (10cm) from the cast-on edge, ending with a wrong-side row.

Starting with a knit row, continue in stockinette stitch until the left front measures 4¾" (12cm) from the cast-on edge, ending with a wrong-side row.

PLACE POCKET

Pocket row K11 (12, 14, 15, 17) stitches, place the next 18 stitches on a holder, k18 stitches along one pocket lining, knit to end.

Continue in stockinette stitch until the left front measures 13¼" (34cm) from the cast-on edge, ending with a wrong-side row.

SHAPE ARMHOLE

Work as for Basic Fitted Cardigan Left Front from Shape Armhole (page 97).

RIGHT FRONT

With size 8 (5mm) needles, cast on 41 (43, 47, 49, 53) stitches.
1st rib row K1, [k2, p2] to last 0 (2, 2, 0, 0) stitches, knit to end.
2nd rib row P0 (2, 2, 0, 0), k2, [p2, k2] to last 3 stitches, p3.
These 2 rows form the rib pattern.
Repeat the last 2 rows until the right front measures 4" (10cm) from the cast-on edge, ending with a wrong-side row.
Starting with a knit row, continue in stockinette stitch until the right front measures 4¾" (12cm) from the cast-on edge, ending with a wrong-side row.

PLACE POCKET

Pocket row K12 (13, 15, 16, 18) stitches, place the next 18 stitches on a holder, k18 stitches along one pocket lining, knit to end.
Continue in stockinette stitch until the right front measures 13¼" (34cm) from the cast-on edge, ending with a right-side row.

SHAPE ARMHOLE

Work as for Basic Fitted Cardigan Right Front from Shape Armhole (page 99).

SLEEVES (MAKE TWO)

With size 8 (5mm) needles, cast on 54 (54, 54, 62, 62) stitches.
Starting with a **1st rib row**, continue in rib pattern until the sleeve measures 2" (5cm) from the cast-on edge, ending with a wrong-side row.
Starting with a knit row, continue in stockinette stitch until the sleeve measures 18" (46cm) from the cast-on edge, ending with a wrong-side row.

SHAPE SLEEVE CAP

Work as for Basic Fitted Cardigan Sleeves from Shape Sleeve Cap (page 99).

LEFT EDGING

With right side facing and size 6 (4mm) needles, pick up and knit 99 stitches down the left front opening edge.
1st rib row [P2, k2] to last 3 stitches, p3.
2nd rib row K3, [p2, k2] to end.
These 2 rows form the rib.
Repeat these 2 rows once.
Work the 1st rib row again.
Bind off.

RIGHT EDGING

With right side facing and size 6 (4mm) needles, pick up and knit 99 stitches up the right front opening edge.
1st rib row P3, [k2, p2] to end.
2nd rib row [K2, p2] to last 3 stitches, k3.
These 2 rows form the rib.
Buttonhole row P3, k2, [p2, k2] twice, *yo, p2tog, k2, [p2, k2] 4 times; repeat from * to last 6 stitches, yo, p2tog, k2, p2.
Work 2 more rows in rib pattern.
Bind off loosely.

NECK EDGING

Join the shoulder seams. With right side facing and size 6 (4mm) needles, pick up and knit 4 stitches from the top of the right buttonhole edging, k11 (11, 12, 12, 13) stitches from the holder at the right front, pick up and k19 (19, 19, 21, 21) stitches up the right front neck, k30 (30, 32, 32, 34) stitches from the holder at the center back, pick up and k19 (19, 19, 21, 21) stitches down the left front neck, k11 (11, 12, 12, 13) stitches from the holder at the left front, pick up and k4 stitches from the top of the left buttonband edging—98 (98, 102, 106, 110) stitches.
Starting with a 2nd rib row as given for the Back, work 2 rows in rib pattern.
Buttonhole row Work in rib pattern to last 4 stitches, yo, k2tog, p2.
Work 2 rows in rib pattern.
Bind off.

POCKET TOPS

Slip 18 stitches from the pocket holder onto size 6 (4mm) needles and rejoin the yarn with right side facing.
Row 1 K1, m1, k1, p2, [k2, p2] to last 2 stitches, k1, m1, k1. 20 stitches.
Row 2 P3, k2, p2, k2, p2tog, yo, k2, p2, k2, p3.
Row 3 K3, [p2, k2] to last stitch, p1.
Row 4 P3, [k2, p2] to last stitch, p1.
Repeat rows 3 and 4.
Bind off.

FINISHING

Sew on the sleeves, placing the center of the sleeves against the shoulder seams. Join the side and sleeve seams. Slip stitch the pocket linings in place. Slip stitch the pocket tops in place. Position and sew the buttons in place.

chevron sleeve cardigan

Even urban looks should have a gentle feminine touch. This carefree cardigan features a lovely striped and chevron pattern in bold colors. Lengthen the chevron pattern for a longer wintery version.

YARN TYPES

YARN

5 (5, 6, 6, 7) balls of Noro Kureyon, 100% wool, 1¾ oz (50g), each approximately 110 yds (100m), shade 154 (A) 🔲 medium

5 (5, 6, 6, 7) balls of Noro Kureyon, 100% wool, 1¾ oz (50g), each approximately 110 yds (100m), shade 164 (B) 🔲 medium

4 buttons size ½" (1.5cm)

NEEDLES
One pair size 8 (5mm) knitting needles or size needed to obtain gauge
One pair size 7 (4.5mm) knitting needles

GAUGE
18 stitches and 24 rows to 4" (10cm) square over stockinette stitch using size 8 (5mm) needles.

MEASUREMENTS
to fit chest

32–34	34–36	36–38	40–42	42–44 inches
81–86	86–91.5	91.5–96.5	101.5–106.5	106.5–111.5cm

actual measurement

35¾	37½	41	43	46¼ inches
91	95.5	104.5	109	117.5cm

length

22	22	22	22¾	22¾ inches
56	56	56	58	58cm

sleeve length

10½	10½	10½	10½	10½ inches
27	27	27	27	27cm

4

4-ROW STRIPED PATTERN

Work 2 rows with A.

Work 2 rows with B.

These 4 rows form the striped pattern; repeat throughout.

BACK

With size 8 (5mm) needles and A, cast on 91 (93, 104, 106, 117) stitches.

1st pattern row (right side) K0 (1, 0, 1, 0), [m1 by knitting into the front and back of next stitch, k4, sl, k2tog, psso, k4, m1] to last 0 (1, 0,1 , 0) stitch, knit to end.

2nd pattern row Purl.

These 2 rows form the chevron pattern.

Repeat the last 2 rows and the striped pattern until the back measures 8½" (22cm) from the cast-on edge, ending with a right-side row.

First, third, and fifth sizes only

Decrease row: P2tog, p4, p2tog, [p11, p2tog] to last 5 stitches, p3, p2tog. 82 (–, 94, –, 106) stitches.

Second and fourth sizes only

Decrease row: P1, [p6, p2tog, p5] to last stitch, p1. – (86, –, 98, –) stitches.

All sizes

Starting with a knit row, continue in stockinette stitch and striped pattern until the back measures 13¼" (34cm) from the cast-on edge, ending with a wrong-side row.

SHAPE ARMHOLES

Work as for Basic Fitted Cardigan Back from Shape Armholes (page 97), working in striped pattern throughout.

LEFT FRONT

With size 8 (5mm) needles and A, cast on 45 (47, 52, 52, 56) stitches.

1st pattern row (right side) K3 (4, 0, 0, 2), [m1 by knitting into the front and back of next stitch, k4, sl, k2tog, psso, k4, m1] to last 3 (4, 0, 0, 2) stitch(es), knit to end.

2nd pattern row Purl.

These 2 rows form the chevron pattern.

Repeat the last 2 rows and the striped pattern until the left front measures 8½" (22cm) from the cast-on edge, ending with a right-side row.

Decrease row [P2tog] 0 (0, 1, 0, 0) times, p2 (3, 10, 12, 14), p2tog, [p11, p2tog] to last 2 (3, 12, 12, 14) stitches, p2 (3,1 0, 12, 14), [p2tog] 0 (0, 1, 0, 0) times. 41 (43, 47 ,49, 53) stitches. Starting with a knit row, continue in stockinette stitch and striped pattern until the left front measures 13¼" (34cm) from the cast-on edge, ending with a wrong-side row.

SHAPE ARMHOLE

Work as for Basic Fitted Cardigan Left Front from Shape Armhole (page 79), working in striped pattern throughout.

RIGHT FRONT

With size 8 (5mm) needles and A, cast on 45 (47, 52, 52, 56) stitches.

1st pattern row (right side) K3 (4, 0, 0, 2), [m1 by knitting into the front and back of next stitch, k4, sl, k2tog, psso, k4, m1] to last 3 (4, 0, 0, 2) stitch(es), knit to end.

2nd pattern row Purl.

These 2 rows form the chevron pattern.

Repeat the last 2 rows and the striped pattern until the right front measures 8½" (22cm) from the cast-on edge, ending with a right-side row.

Decrease row [P2tog] 0 (0, 1, 0, 0) times, p2 (3, 10, 12, 14), p2tog, [p11, p2tog] to last 2 (3, 12, 12, 14) stitches, p2 (3,1 0, 12, 14), [p2tog] 0 (0, 1, 0, 0) times. 41 (43, 47 ,49, 53) stitches. Starting with a knit row, continue in stockinette stitch and striped pattern until the right front measures 13¼" (34cm) from the cast-on edge, ending with a right-side row.

SHAPE ARMHOLE

Work as for Basic Fitted Cardigan Right Front from Shape Armhole (page 99), working in striped pattern throughout.

SLEEVES (MAKE TWO)

With size 8 (5mm) needles and A, cast on 65 (65, 65, 78, 78) stitches.

1st pattern row (right side) [M1 by knitting into the front and back of next stitch, k4, sl, k2tog, psso, k4, m1] to end.

2nd pattern row Purl.

These 2 rows form the chevron pattern.

Repeat the last 2 rows and the striped pattern until the sleeve measures 6" (15cm) from the cast-on edge, ending with a right-side row.

First, second, and third sizes only

Decrease row P2tog, p3, s1, p2tog, psso, *p10, s1, p2tog, psso; repeat from * to last 5 stitches, p5. 54 (54, 54, –, –) stitches.

Fourth and fifth sizes only

Decrease row P1, p2tog, [p3, p2tog] to end. –(–, –, 62, 62) stitches.

All sizes

Starting with a knit row, continue in stockinette stitch and striped pattern until the sleeve measures 10½" (27cm) from the cast-on edge, ending with a wrong-side row.

SHAPE SLEEVE CAP
Complete as for Basic Fitted Cardigan Sleeves from Shape Sleeve Cap (page 99), working in striped pattern throughout.

LEFT EDGING
With right side facing, using size 7 (4.5mm) needles and A, pick up and knit 95 stitches down the left front opening edge.
Knit 6 rows.
Bind off.

RIGHT EDGING
With right side facing, using size 7 (4.5mm) needles and yarn A, pick up and knit 95 stitches up the right front opening edge.
1st, 2nd, and 3rd rows Knit to end.
4th row K61, [bind off 2 stitches, knit until there are 10 stitches on the right needle after bind off] twice, bind off 2 stitches, knit to end.
5th row K8, [cast on 2 stitches, k10] twice, cast on 2 stitches, knit to end.
6th row Knit to end.
Bind off.

NECK EDGING
Join the shoulder seams. With right side facing, using size 7 (4.5mm) needles and A, pick up and k4 stitches from the top of the right buttonhole edging, k11 (11, 12, 12, 13) stitches from the holder at the right front, pick up and k19 (19, 19, 21, 21) stitches up the right front neck, k30 (30, 32, 32, 34) stitches from the holder at the center back, pick up and k19 (19, 19, 21, 21) stitches down the left front neck, k11 (11, 12, 12, 13) stitches from the holder at the left front, pick up and k4 stitches from the top of the left buttonband edging—98 (98, 102, 106, 110) stitches.
1st row Knit to end.
2nd row K2, bind off 2 stitches, knit to end.
3rd row Knit to last 2 stitches, cast on 2 sts, knit to end.
4th row Knit to end.
Bind off.

FINISHING
Sew on the sleeves, placing the center of the sleeves against the shoulder seams. Join the side and sleeve seams. Position and sew the buttons in place.

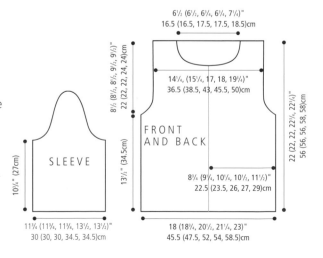

6½ (6½, 6¾, 6¾, 7¼)"
16.5 (16.5, 17.5, 17.5, 18.5)cm

14¼, (15¼, 17, 18, 19¾)"
36.5 (38.5, 43, 45.5, 50)cm

8½ (8½, 8½, 9½, 9½)"
22 (22, 22, 24, 24)cm

13½" (34.5cm)

10¼" (27cm)

SLEEVE

FRONT AND BACK

22 (22, 22, 22¼, 22¾)"
56 (56, 56, 58, 58)cm

8¾ (9¼, 10¼, 10½, 11½)"
22.5 (23.5, 26, 27, 29)cm

11¾ (11¾, 11¾, 13½, 13½)"
30 (30, 30, 34.5, 34.5)cm

18 (18¾, 20½, 21¼, 23)"
45.5 (47.5, 52, 54, 58.5)cm

thick-ribbed cardigan

Get set for autumn in this super-cool knit. Thick ribbing, softly contoured shape, and deep saturated hues gives this feminine piece a street-smart edge. Collar can be zipped up or rolled down.

YARN TYPES

YARN
8 (8, 9, 9, 10) balls of Noro Silk Garden, 45% silk/45% mohair/10% lambswool, 1¾oz (50g), each approximately 110 yds (100m), shade 201 (4) medium

Open-ended zipper to fit:
First 3 sizes: length 24" (61cm)
Last 2 sizes: length 25" (63cm)

NEEDLES
One pair size 8 (5mm) knitting needles or size needed to obtain gauge
One pair size 6 (4mm) knitting needles

GAUGE
18 stitches and 24 rows to 4" (10cm) square over rib pattern when slightly stretched, using size 8 (5mm) needles.

MEASUREMENTS
to fit chest

32–34	34–36	36–38	40–42	42–44 inches
81–86	86–91.5	91.5–96.5	101.5–106.5	106.5–111.5cm

actual measurement

35¾	37½	41	43	46¼ inches
91	95.5	104.5	109	117.5cm

length

24½	24½	24½	25¼	25¼ inches
62	62	62	64	64cm

sleeve length

18	18	18	18	18 inches
46	46	46	46	46cm

BACK

With size 8 (5mm) needles, cast on 82 (86, 94, 98, 106) stitches.

1st rib row K2, [p2, k2] to end.
2nd rib row P2, [k2, p2] to end.
These 2 rows form the rib pattern.
Repeat the last 2 rows until the back measures 15¾" (40cm) from the cast-on edge, ending with a wrong-side row.

SHAPE ARMHOLES

Work as for Basic Fitted Cardigan Back from Shape Armholes (page 97), working in rib pattern throughout.

LEFT FRONT

With size 8 (5mm) needles, cast on 41 (43, 47, 49, 53) stitches.

1st rib row K0 (1, 1, 0, 0), p1 (2, 2, 1, 1), [k2, p2] to last 4 stitches, k4.
2nd rib row [K2, p2] to last 1 (3, 3, 1, 1) stitch(es), k1 (2, 2, 1, 1), p0 (1, 1, 0, 0).
These 2 rows form the rib pattern with the edge 2 stitches in garter stitch.
Repeat the last 2 rows until the left front measures 15¾" (40cm) from the cast-on edge, ending with a wrong-side row.

SHAPE ARMHOLE

Work as for Basic Fitted Cardigan Left Front from Shape Armhole (page 97), working in rib pattern throughout.

RIGHT FRONT

With size 8 (5mm) needles, cast on 41 (43, 47, 49, 53) stitches.

1st rib row K4, [p2, k2] to last 1 (3, 3, 1, 1) stitch(es), p1 (2, 2, 1, 1), k0 (1, 1, 0, 0).
2nd rib row P0 (1, 1, 0, 0), k1 (2 ,2, 1,1), [p2, k2] to end.
These 2 rows form the rib pattern, with the edge stitches in garter stitch.
Repeat the last 2 rows until the right front measures 15¾" (40cm) from the cast-on edge, ending with a right-side row.

SHAPE ARMHOLE

Work as for Basic Fitted Cardigan Right Front from Shape Armhole (page 99), working in rib pattern throughout.

SLEEVES (MAKE TWO)

Starting with a **1st rib row** as given for the Back, work as for Basic Fitted Cardigan Sleeves (page 99), working in rib throughout.

COLLAR

Join the shoulder seams. With right side facing and using size 8 (5mm) needles, k11 (11, 12, 12, 13) stitches from the holder at the right front, pick up and k13 (13, 13, 15, 15) stitches up the right front neck, k30 (30, 32, 32, 34) stitches from the holder at the center back, pick up and k13 (13, 13, 15, 15) stitches down the left front neck, k11 (11, 12, 12, 13) stitches from the holder at the left front—78 (78, 82, 86, 90) stitches.
Next row K2, [p2, k2] to end.
Next row K4, [p2, k2] to last 2 stitches, k2.
Repeat the last 2 rows until the collar measures 4¾" (12cm) from the pick-up row, ending with a wrong-side row.
Bind off.

FINISHING

Sew on the sleeves, placing the center of the sleeves against the shoulder seams. Join the side and sleeve seams. Position and sew the zipper in place.

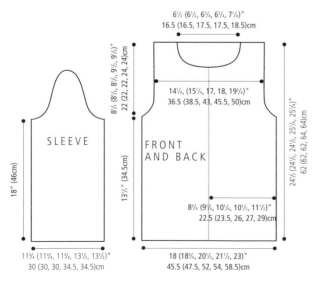

6½ (6½, 6¾, 6¼, 7¼)"
16.5 (16.5, 17.5, 17.5, 18.5)cm

8½ (8½, 8½, 9½, 9½)"
22 (22, 22, 24, 24)cm

14¼, (15¼, 17, 18, 19¾)"
36.5 (38.5, 43, 45.5, 50)cm

SLEEVE

FRONT AND BACK

13½" (34.5cm)

24½ (24½, 24½, 25¼, 25¼)"
62 (62, 62, 64, 64)cm

18" (46cm)

8¾ (9¼, 10¼, 10½, 11½)"
22.5 (23.5, 26, 27, 29)cm

11¾ (11¾, 11¾, 13½, 13½)"
30 (30, 30, 34.5, 34.5)cm

18 (18¼, 20½, 21¼, 23)"
45.5 (47.5, 52, 54, 58.5)cm

WRAPS

basic wrap

Bold variegated yarns knitted up in blocks of pure color can make a statement in itself. Team it with a unique stitch pattern and you have yourself a design to be reckoned with! This chapter transforms basic rectangular shapes into a variety of soft and feminine cover-ups, from this lace scarf to a delicate top.

YARN TYPES

YARN
9 balls of Noro Silk Garden, 45% silk/45% mohair/10% lambswool, 1¾ oz (50g), each approximately 110 yds (100m), shade 2011 (4) medium

NEEDLES
One pair size 6 (4mm) knitting needles or size needed to obtain gauge

GAUGE
20 stitches and 28 rows to 4" (10cm) square over pattern using size 8 (5mm) needles.

MEASUREMENTS
22½ x 61" (57 x 155cm)

TO MAKE
With size 6 (4mm) needles, cast on 114 stitches.
Knit 5 rows.
1st pattern row (wrong side) K5, [p4, k4] to last 5 stitches, p4, k1.
2nd pattern row Knit.
Repeat the last 2 rows twice more.
Knit 4 rows.
11th pattern row K1, p4, [k4, p4] to last 5 stitches, k5.
12th pattern row Knit.
Repeat the last 2 rows twice more.
Knit 4 rows.
These 20 rows form the pattern
Repeat the last 20 rows until the work measures approximately 61" (155cm) from the cast-on edge, ending with a 20th pattern row.
Bind off.

22½" (57cm)

61" (155cm)

1

shawl

This sumptuous shawl is perfect for weekend jaunts into the country. An allover basketweave pattern is balanced out with garter-stitch detailing along the edges, which also helps prevent it from curling.

YARN TYPES

YARN
6 balls of Noro Cashmere Island, 60% wool/30% cashmere/ 10% nylon, 1¾ oz (50g), each approximately 137 yds (125m), in shade 10 (3) light

NEEDLES
One pair size 6 (4mm) knitting needles or size needed to obtain gauge

GAUGE
20 stitches and 21 rows to 4" (10cm) square over pattern using size 6 (4mm) needles.

MEASUREMENTS
15¼ x 61" (38.5 x 155cm)

TO MAKE
With size 6 (4mm) needles, cast on 77 stitches.
1st pattern row (right side) K1, yo, s1, k2tog, psso, [yo, k1, yo, s1, k2tog, psso] to last stitch, yo, k1.
2nd and 4th pattern rows Purl.
3rd pattern row K1, yo, k2tog, [yo, s1, k2tog, psso, yo, k1] to last 3 stitches, yo, s1, k1, psso.
These 4 rows form the lace pattern.
Repeat the last 4 rows until the shawl measures 61" (155cm)
Bind off.

15¼" (38.5cm)

61" (155cm)

lace cover-up

With simple lines and hazy tones, this little cover-up is the personification of modern pretty. Quite unique, it's knit sideways in a rectangular lace pattern and trimmed with ribbed edging. A one-button closure makes it extra sweet.

3

YARN

5 (5, 6, 6, 7) balls of Noro Cashmere Island, 60% wool/30% cashmere/10% nylon, 1¾ oz (50g), each approximately 137 yds (125m), shade 12 ⬛ light

One button size ½" (1.5cm)

NEEDLES

One pair size 6 (4mm) knitting needles or size needed to obtain gauge
One pair size 5 (3.75mm) knitting needles

GAUGE

20 stitches and 26 rows to 4" (10cm) square over pattern using size 6 (4mm) needles.

MEASUREMENTS

to fit chest

extra small	small	medium	large	extra large
32	34	36	38	40 inches
81.5	86.5	91.5	96.5	101.5cm

actual measurement

36¼	38½	41¾	44	47¼ inches
92	98	106	112	120cm

length

18½	18½	18½	18½	18½ inches
47	47	47	47	47cm

BACK

With size 6 (4mm) needles, cast on 94 stitches.
1st pattern row (right side) K2, yo, s1, k2tog, psso, [yo, k1, yo, s1, k2tog, psso] to last stitch, yo, k1.
2nd and 4th pattern rows Purl.
3rd pattern row K2, yo, k2tog, [yo, s1, k2tog, psso, yo, k1] to last 2 stitches, yo, s1, k1, psso.
These 4 rows form the lace pattern.
Repeat the last 4 rows until the back measures 18 (19¼, 21, 22, 23½)" (46 [49, 53, 56, 60]cm) from the cast-on edge, ending with a wrong-side row.
Bind off.

LEFT FRONT

With size 6 (4mm) needles, cast on 94 stitches.
Starting with a **1st pattern row** as given for the back, continue in lace pattern until the left front measures 8½ (9, 9¾, 10½, 11½)" (22 [23, 25, 27, 29]cm) from the cast-on edge,
ending with a wrong-side row.
1st rib row K2, [p2, k2] to end.
2nd rib row P2, [k2, p2] to end.
These 2 rows form the rib pattern.
Repeat the last 2 rows until left front measures 9½ (9¾, 10½, 11½, 12)" (24 [25, 27, 29, 31]cm) from the cast-on edge, ending with a wrong-side row.
Bind off.

RIGHT FRONT

With size 6 (4mm) needles, cast on 94 stitches.
Starting with a **1st rib row** as given for the left front, work 2 rows, ending with a wrong-side row.
Buttonhole row K2, p2tog, yo, rib to end.
Continue in rib pattern until the right front measures ¾" (2cm) from the cast-on edge, ending with a wrong-side row.
Starting with a **1st pattern row** as given for the back, continue in lace pattern until the right front measures 9½ (9¾, 10½, 11½, 12)" (24 [25, 27, 29, 31]cm) from the cast-on edge, ending with a wrong-side row.
Bind off.

ARMHOLE EDGING

Join the shoulder seams by sewing 4" (10cm) in from the upper right-hand and upper left-hand edges. Place markers 7¾ (7¾, 7¾, 8¼, 8¼)" (20 [20, 20, 21, 21]cm) down the sides from the shoulder seam. With right side facing and size 5 (3.75mm) needles, pick up and k37 (37, 37, 43, 43) stitches from the marker up one side of the armhole edge, pick up and k37 (37, 37, 43, 43) stitches down the other side of armhole edge to the marker—74 (74, 74, 86, 86) stitches.
Rib 6 rows.
Bind off.

FINISHING

Join the side and armhole edging seams. Position and sew the button in place.

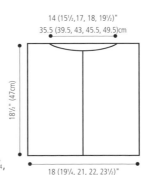

14 (15½, 17, 18, 19½)"
35.5 (39.5, 43, 45.5, 49.5)cm

18½" (47cm)

18 (19¼, 21, 22, 23½)"
46 (49, 53, 56, 60)cm

YARN TYPES

YARN

9 (9, 10) 50g balls of Noro Silk Garden Lite, 45% silk/45% mohair/10% lambswool, 1¾ oz (50g), each approximately 110 yds (100m), shade 2010  medium

NEEDLES

One pair size 6 (4mm) knitting needles or size needed to obtain gauge
One pair size 5 (3.75mm) knitting needles

GAUGE

22 stitches and 30 rows to 4" (10cm) square over pattern using size 6 (4mm) needles.

MEASUREMENTS

to fit chest

small	medium	large
32–34	36–40	42–46 inches
81.5–86.5	91.5–101.5	106.5–117cm

actual measurement

39¼	45¾	52 inches
100	116	132.5cm

length

29½	29½	30¾ inches
75	75	78cm

chevron top

There's a gorgeous femininity in this short-sleeve Chevron Top. The sleeves are knit as part of the body for fuss-free finishing. A beautiful rainbow-hued ribbing outlines the garment's edges.

4

BACK

With size 6 (4mm) needles, cast on 110 (128, 146) stitches.

1st and 4th pattern rows Knit.

2nd pattern row (wrong side) Purl.

3rd pattern row K1, *[k2tog] 3 times, [yo, k1] 6 times, [k2tog] 3 times, repeat from * to last stitch, k1.

These 4 rows form the lace pattern.

Repeat the last 4 rows until back measures 29½ (29½, 30¾)" (75 [75, 78]cm) from the cast-on edge, ending with a wrong-side row.

SHAPE SHOULDERS

Bind off 29 (38, 47) stitches at the beginning of the next 2 rows. Leave the center 52 stitches on a holder.

LEFT FRONT

With size 6 (4mm) needles, cast on 29 (38, 47) stitches.

1st and 4th pattern row Knit.

2nd pattern row (wrong side) Purl.

3rd pattern row [K2tog] 3 (0, 3) times, [yo, k1] 3 (0, 3) times, *[k2tog] 3 times, [yo, k1] 6 times, [k2tog] 3 times; repeat from * to last 2 stitches, knit to end.

These 4 rows form the lace pattern.

Repeat the last 4 rows until the left front measures 29½ (29½, 30¾)" (75 [75, 78]cm) from the cast-on edge, ending with a wrong-side row.

Bind off.

RIGHT FRONT

With size 6 (4mm) needles, cast on 29 (38, 47) stitches.

1st and 4th pattern row Knit.

2nd pattern row (wrong side) Purl.

3rd pattern row K2, *[k2tog] 3 times, [yo, k1] 6 times, [k2tog] 3 times; repeat from * to last 9 (0, 9) stitches, [yo, k1] 3 (0, 3) times, [k2tog] 3 (0, 3) times.

These 4 rows form the lace pattern.

Repeat the last 4 rows until the right front measures 29½ (29½, 30¾)" (75 [75, 78]cm) from the cast-on edge, ending with a wrong-side row.

Bind off.

RIGHT EDGING

Join the shoulder seams. With right side facing and size 5 (3.75mm) needles, pick up and k196 (196, 200) stitches up the right front opening edge, knit 26 stitches across the back neck to center back neck—222 (222, 226) stitches.

1st rib row (wrong side) [K2, p2] to end.

2nd rib row [K2, p2] to end.

Repeat the last 2 rows until the edging measures 2½" (6cm), ending with a wrong-side row.

Bind off loosely in rib pattern.

LEFT EDGING

With right side facing and size 5 (3.75mm) needles, k26 stitches across the back neck from center back neck, pick up and k196 (196, 200) stitches down the left front opening edge—222 (222, 226) stitches.

1st rib row (wrong side) [P2, k2] to end.

2nd rib row [K2, p2] to end.

Repeat the last 2 rows until the edging measures 2½" (6cm), ending with a wrong-side row.

Bind off loosely in rib pattern.

ARMHOLE EDGING

Join the shoulder seams. Place markers 7¾ (8¼, 8½)" (20 [21, 22]cm) down the sides from each shoulder seam. With right side facing and size 5 (3.75mm) needles, pick up and k49 (53, 57) stitches up one side of the armhole edge from marker, pick up and k49 (53, 57) stitches down the other side of armhole edge to marker—98 (106, 114) stitches.

1st rib row (wrong side) P2, [k2, p2] to end.

2nd rib row K2, [p2, k2] to end.

Repeat the last 2 rows until the edging measures 1¼" (3cm), ending with a wrong-side row.

Bind off loosely in rib pattern.

Repeat for other armhole.

FINISHING

Join the edging together at the center back neck. Join the side and armhole edging seams.

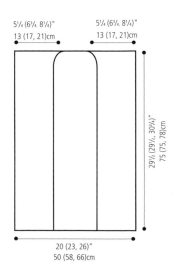

5¼ (6¼, 8¼)" 13 (17, 21)cm   5¼ (6¼, 8¼)" 13 (17, 21)cm

29½ (29½, 30¾)" 75 (75, 78)cm

20 (23, 26)" 50 (58, 66)cm

paneled top

This decidedly cool and abstract top is incredibly easy to knit. Simply create a tube of stockinette-stitched fabric and add ribbing to the waist. For a more elaborate project, knit a flare skirt just below the ribbed waistline.

YARN

7 (7, 8, 8) balls of Noro Cashmere Island, 60% wool/30% cashmere/10% nylon, 1¾ oz (50g), each approximately 137 yds (125m), shade 11 ![4] medium

NEEDLES

One pair size 6 (4mm) knitting needles or size needed to obtain gauge
One pair size 5 (3.75mm) knitting needles or size needed to obtain gauge

GAUGE

21 stitches and 30 rows to 4" (10cm) square over stockinette stitch using size 6 (4mm) needles.
20 stitches and 30 rows to 4" (10cm) square over rib when stretched using size 5 (3.75mm) needles.

MEASUREMENTS

to fit chest

extra small	small	medium	large
32–34	36–38	38–40	40–42 inches
81.5–86.5	91.5–96.5	96.5–101.5	101.5–106.5cm

actual measurement

31½	33¼	35½	38 inches
80.5	84.5	90.5	96.5cm

length

19¾	19¾	19¾	19¾ inches
50	50	50	50cm

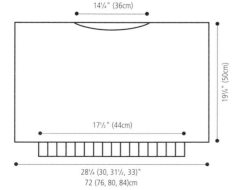

14¼" (36cm)

19¾" (50cm)

17½" (44cm)

28¼ (30, 31½, 33)"
72 (76, 80, 84)cm

Note

This garment is knit sideways.

BACK

With size 6 (4mm) needles, cast on 85 stitches.
Knit 3 rows.
1st row Knit.
2nd row Purl to last 3 stitches, knit to end.
Repeat the last 2 rows until the back measures 28¼ (30, 31½, 33)" 72 (76, 80, 84]cm) from the cast-on edge, ending with a wrong-side row.
Knit 3 rows.
Bind off.

FRONT

With size 6 (4mm) needles, cast on 85 stitches.
Knit 3 rows.
1st row Knit.
2nd row K3, purl to end.
Repeat the last 2 rows until the front measures 28¼ (30, 31½, 33)" (72 [76, 80, 84]cm) from the cast-on edge, ending with a wrong-side row.
Knit 3 rows.
Bind off.

EDGING

The garter stitch edge is the top of the garment. Place markers 7 (7¾, 8½, 9½)" (18 [20, 22, 24]cm) in from each top edge. Working from the markers to the edges, join the shoulder seams. Place markers 5½ (6¼, 7, 7¾)" (14 [16, 18, 20]cm) in from each bottom edge. Join the right sleeve seam by working from the marker to the edge. With right side facing and size 5 (3.75mm) needles, and starting at the marker at the left sleeve seam, pick up and k80 (84, 90, 96) stitches along the bottom front edge and pick up and k81 (85, 91, 97) stitches along the bottom back edge back to the marker—161 (169, 181, 193) stitches.
1st rib row (wrong side) P1, [k1, p1] to end.
2nd rib row K1, [p1, k1] to end.
These 2 rows form the rib pattern.
Repeat the last two rows until the edging measures 4" (10cm), ending with a wrong-side row.
Bind off.

FINISHING

Join the left sleeve seam by working from the marker to the edge. Join the edging seam.

where to find noro yarns

Noro yarns are distributed in the U.S. by Knitting Fever and are available at fine stores across the country. To find a store near you, go to www.knittingfever.com and use their store locator, or visit one of the stores below. Be sure to call ahead to confirm the desired yarn and color is in stock before you make the trip.

Halcyon Yarn, Inc.
12 School St.
Bath, ME 04530
(920) 744-2790
www.halcyonyarn.com

Imagiknit
3897 18th St.
San Francisco, CA 94114
(415) 621-6642
www.imagiknit.com

Knit Happens
N. 127-A Washington St.
Alexandria, VA 22314
(703) 836-0039
www.knithappens.net

Knit New York, Inc.
307 E. 14th St.
New York, NY 10003
(212) 387-0707
www.knitnewyork.com

Knitch
1052 St. Charles Ave.
Atlanta, GA 30306
(404) 745-YARN
www.shopknitch.com

La Knitterie Parisienne
12642 Ventura Blvd.
Studio City, CA 91604
(800) 2-BUY-YARN
www.laknitterieparisienne.net

Royal Yarns
404 Barnside Pl.
Rockville, MD 20850
(202) 215-2300
www.royalyarns.com

Sit 'n Knit
10 LaSalle Rd.
West Hartford, CT 06107
(860) 232-YARN
www.sit-n-knit.com

Tricoter
3121 E. Madison St.
Suite 104
Seattle, WA 98112
(206) 328-6505
www.tricoter.com

Webs
75 Service Center Rd.
Northampton, MA 01060
(800) 367-9327
www.yarn.com

The Yarn Basket
150 Falling Spring Rd.
Chambersburg, PA 17201
(888) 976-2758
www.yarnbasketpa.com

The Yarn and Fiber Co.
58 Range Rd.
Windham, NH 03087
(603) 898-5059
www.yarnandfiber.com

Yarn Garden
1413 S. E. Hawthorne Blvd.
Portland, OR 97214
(503) 239-7950
www.yarngarden.net

Yarn Paradise
6 All Souls Crescent
Asheville, NC 28803
(828) 274-4213
www.yarnparadise.com

Yarnbow
1607 Ranch Rd. 620 N.
Suite 800
Austin, TX 78734
(512) 535-2332
www.yarnbow.com

YarnMarket.com
(888) 996-YARN
www.yarnmarket.com

yarn standards

The Yarn Council of America have a system of categorizing yarns that you may find useful. It provides a guide only and you should always use the gauge and needle size given in a pattern you are following.

yarn weight symbol	yarn category names	recommended US (metric) needle size	gauge range in stockinette stitch over 4" (10cm)
0 LACE	10-count crochet thread (fingering)	000–1 (1.5–2.25mm)	33–40 sts
1 SUPER FINE	Sock, baby (fingering)	1–2 (2.25–3.25mm)	27–32 sts
2 FINE	Lightweight DK, baby (sport)	3–5 (3.25–3.75mm)	23–26 sts
3 LIGHT	DK (light worsted)	5–7 (3.75–4.5mm)	21–24 sts
4 MEDIUM	Aran (worsted, afghan)	7–9 (4.5–5.5mm)	16–20 sts
5 BULKY	Chunky (craft, rug)	9–11 (5.5–8mm)	12–15 sts
6 SUPER BULKY	Bulky, roving	11 and larger (8mm and larger)	6–11 sts

abbreviations

k knit
k2tog knit 2 stitches together
m1 make 1 stitch by picking up the loop lying between the stitch just worked and next stitch and working into the back of it
p purl
p2tog purl 2 stitches together
psso pass slipped stitch over
RS right side
s1 slip 1 stitch

st(s) stitch(es)
T2K knit into back of 2nd stitch, then knit into front of 1st stitch and slip both stitches off needle together
T2P purl into front of 2nd stitch, then purl into front of 1st stitch and slip both stitches off needle together
tbl through back loop
tog together
WS wrong side
yo yarn over